Collector's Encyclopedia of

FIGURAL PLANTERS & VASES

Identification & Values

Betty & Bill Newbound

COLLECTOR BOOKS
A Division of Schroeder Publishing Co., Inc.

The current values of this book should be used only as a guide. They are not intended to set prices, which vary from one section of the country to another. Auction prices as well as dealer prices vary greatly and are affected by condition as well as demand. Neither the Authors nor the Publisher assumes responsibility for any losses that might be incurred as a result of consulting this guide.

Searching for a Publisher?

We are always looking for knowledgeable people considered to be experts within their fields. If you feel that there is a real need for a book on your collectible subject and have a large comprehensive collection, contact Collector Books.

Cover Design: Karen Geary
Book Design: Donna Ballard
Photos: Bill Newbound

On the cover:

Dutch couple with a wishing well	$25.00 – 30.00
Clown with a vase	$15.00 – 20.00
Bunny in a garden	$7.00 – 9.00
Donkey and elephant at the well	$40.00 – 45.00

Printed in the U.S.A. by Image Graphics

Contents

# Dedication

For our granddaughter, Cydney – who loves to "garden" in her Mom's flower pots.

 # Acknowledgments and Thanks

Our heartfelt thanks to all those who helped us with this book by lending pottery, by allowing us to take photos in their antiques malls and in their homes and even letting us stay with them while photographing.

To Sherry Clair, who gave us the idea in the first place. To Yvonne Groat, Jill Gibbs, John Wanat, Karla Kiikka, Bob and Dot MacIntyre, Sue Goldhardt and Tom Jerpbak of Ye Old Oaken Bucket Antiques, Joel Steiner Martin and Mason Bright of the American Heritage Antiques Mall, Daphene and Bob Hansor, Norma and Sherman Lilly, and our daughter, Emalee, who gave us a bed to sleep in, fed us, and lugged us to all the Tiffin Flea Markets in search of planters. Also a special thanks to Jimmy Tafoya who loaned us a camera when ours gave up at a critical point.

Thank you all so much – we couldn't have done it without you!

A Sliver of History

I wonder who it was who looked one day at a plain terra cotta flower pot and thought "Well, this is dull; what can we do to liven it up?" Was it a potter yearning to "do something different" or a designer just doodling on his sketch pad who suddenly found he'd created a new product? We'll probably never know.

Did the first cavewomen bring handfuls of flowers into their dull, one-color caves, I wonder? When did the desire for beauty first emerge in human beings? Flowers and foliage have been important accents in our homes for many, many years. A lot of attention has always been paid to the containers in which the flowers and plants are displayed. From primitive, folk pottery jugs and pots to fabulous art pottery, to Great-grandma's ubiquitous fern stand, folks have always had an eye toward brightening their homes with plants and flowers placed in interesting and attractive containers. From about 1940 – 1970, figural planters and vases were hot. I can recall seeing shelves packed with them in our local dime store. They were a favorite little gift for Mom or Grandma back when I thought I was doing pretty well in our small town making $35.00 a week. You could buy a nice planter for 39¢ – 59¢, go to the local greenhouse and buy a small plant for about 50¢ and they would even plant it for you!

Today, these whimsical little planters and vases with their appealing little people and animal figures are becoming popular again. This time collectors are avidly hunting them at flea markets, antiques shops and malls and garage sales. Once again, these little objects are doing their jobs, brightening homes across the country.

The Life Story of Your Planter or Vase

Figural planters and vases are, for the most part, made with the same techniques that are used in the production of any china or ceramic hollowware. Everything begins with the designer who can be someone employed by the pottery or a representative from an importer or exporter. This designer supplies the pottery with information about how he sees the piece. He provides sketches of the piece along with suggestions on size, decoration, etc. These are referred to a sculptor who carves the piece out of a block of special modeling clay. This is the time when a mark or logo is carved into the base of the piece if desired. This model is taken to the pottery's mold maker. A mold of the piece is made by suspending the piece in a container of liquid latex which is allowed to harden. When sufficiently hardened, the model is removed and split in half. The sculpted piece is removed leaving the reverse image of the piece in latex. Samples are made from this for the approval of the pottery or importer. After approval, production molds are made from a very hard plaster of paris type material.

Many planters and vases have what is called a dry foot on the bottom of the piece. This varies in shape from pottery to pottery and may consist of "wedges" as in American Bisque ware, or "bars" as in Royal Copley/Spaulding. This foot is left with no glaze so that when the item is fired it will not stick to the kiln floor or shelf. If the piece is made with a glazed bottom, it will be necessary to place three or four unglazed bisque "stilts" to keep the glaze from adhering to the kiln floor. These form the "stilt marks" or little, unglazed circles or squares often found on the bottom of ceramic items.

The raw materials used for the body of the planter or vase vary. Feldspar, flint, and talc are mainly used in this country, along with various clays that fire in different colors such as white, rusty red or gray. These materials are measured and weighed in the correct proportions and mixed for perhaps an hour in a mixing machine. After several screening processes, the result is liquid clay called slip. This slip is poured into the plaster molds and allowed to set for a time. Knowing how long to leave the slip in the mold comes with years of experience in the pottery business. When the desired wall thickness of the piece is achieved, the excess slip is poured out and dumped back into the mixers for reuse. After more drying time, the mold is opened and the item removed and allowed to air dry. The piece at this point is tough and leathery in consistency and small cracks and other defects can be repaired. Excess material on the edges is pared off with a special knife and pieces are smoothed with a wet sponge or other tool.

When the item is completely dry, it is known as "greenware." If any ornament or handle is to be attached to the main body of the piece, it will be done now using a special bonding material. Also, if the vase or planter does not sit flat, more scraping, paring or trimming may be necessary. This extra step results in planters from the same pottery sometimes having different-looking bases.

The next step is decorating, using various methods. In the case of inexpensive planters, a transparent glaze is applied directly to the greenware and colors applied over that. After decorating, the item is fired. In the case of more expensive pieces, the item is fired, decorated, glazed, and fired again. Glaze can be glossy or matte (dull).

The main decorating methods used on figural planters and vases are air brushing, hand painting, colored slip, and applied or "sprigged-on" decoration and decals. Often there is a combination of several of these. In air brushing, a spray gun the size of a pen or pencil is used instead of a brush. The small gun has an attached container for paint and each gun is attached to an air supply. Adjustable nozzles which make it possible for the decorator to control the paint flow are on the end of the gun. Air brushing is generally used to cover larger areas with a color or sometimes to swirl together or shade several colors. After the larger areas are painted, hand decorators add features, gold lining, and other trim.

Do not get the notion that if you chip a solid color planter it won't show because the planter is that color all the way through. No, no, no! Several potteries did try producing solid-color pieces in the 1940s when plain-colored dinnerware suddenly became the rage. However, after experimenting for some time,

they found it did not work. Colors could not be controlled and came out blotchy and uneven. The plain-colored planters and vases are actually decorated or coated with a colored slip. If they chip, they will be white inside, or whatever color the base clay is.

Applied, or as the potters call it "sprigged-on" decoration is the process of applying small molded pieces to the surface of the item using slip or liquid clay or a special bonding glue. Particular care must be taken that the small item has the same degree of shrinkage as the body or the small piece may break off before or during firing. These small pieces are sometimes found with gold accents or even, as in some newer planters, dusted with glitter. In the case of the more delicate and detailed ladies, arms and hands are often made and applied separately. The same goes for some hats, baskets, etc., depending on the design of the piece. Ruffles are sometimes molded in and sometimes pressed onto the piece separately using clay of a consistency much the same as a cake decorator's frosting. The delicate, applied flowers found on various planters and vases are made using the same methods a cake decorator would use to build up a flower petal by petal. After drying, these are then applied to the main body of the piece.

You will find a few planters or vases decorated with decals, especially the type with mottoes or a fair amount of writing, such as the open books shown in the Objects chapter. To make a decal, a printing press prints the design on the sticky side of gummed paper, using a type of varnish instead of ink. Then, the colored design or writing is printed on top of the previously printed varnish. The varnish area makes a base for the colors, which are printed with ceramic inks. The decals are then cut into units. To apply, the decal is placed in water which softens the gum. Then the design on its film of varnish is slid off the paper and placed on the pottery, either bisque or glazed.

Hand painting will be found on some planters and vases, but mostly as accents added after air brushing or colored slip coating. Gold lining or trim is done with a solution of gold chloride under the glaze. When reheated in the kiln, the solution burns off to leave the bright gold. If your trim is silver in color (unusual), the medium used is actually platinum since real silver burns to a straw color in the kiln. Today, any planter or vase with gold trim in good condition brings a higher price than its less highly-decorated companions. Hand painting could be done on the bisque ware and then covered with the glaze, or the method of painting over the glaze could be used. This saved at least one firing and was a less expensive way of doing things. When this over-the-glaze paint is not fired at all, it is referred to as "cold painting," and the result will wear off much more quickly than the underglaze style of decoration.

The Care of Ceramic Planters & Vases

First, keep in mind that you are not buying a new item off the local department store shelf — you are buying used, "second-hand-rose" items and most will not be in mint condition! You need to decide how much grunge and possible damage are acceptable to you. Of course, you will not pay full price for damaged pieces. Crazing will reduce the value of your piece very little unless the craze is very deep, rough, and/or stained. Pieces that have been decorated by the cold paint method will almost always have worn-off spots from being used and washed often. Personally, I feel that it is OK to replace, with care, any worn cold paint. Naturally, if you ever sell the piece, it should be labeled "re-painted" or "touched-up."

Examine your planter or vase to determine if the decoration, if any, is applied over or under the glaze. If the colors are underglaze, you can be tougher with your cleaning procedures. Overglaze colors will scratch off, or melt off, so do not use steel wool or plastic scrubbies! Bar Keepers Friend™, a good but gentle cleaning powder, can safely be used on underglaze colors with no harm done. But *not* on gold! Gold trim is risky because it is often thinly applied. Also, the nature of gold is that it will sometimes change color depending on the chemical content of cleaners used on it. For gold trimmed pieces, use mild detergent, warm water, and a soft sponge or brush. Sometimes stains can be removed with a little lemon juice. If your vase or planter is much crazed (well,

you liked it so much, you bought it anyway, right?), you will have to be more careful in cleaning since super strong methods may cause pieces of glaze to flake off. I've never had this happen myself, but have heard horror stories about it!

A great many of the planters and vases we find at sales and markets have an accumulation of lime or other mineral residue inside which is, of course, a result of using the vase or planter for live plants. Sometimes they even still have the dirt in them. If either is the case, first soak the piece in warm soapy water for a couple of hours. Then scrub inside with a brush to remove dirt and rinse, rinse, rinse. If there is still a mineral deposit inside, and there probably will be, try filling the cavity with a toilet bowl cleaner such as Sno Bowl™.

Generally, the cleaner, used straight from the bottle, will foam up around the mineral. You may have to leave the planter to soak for several hours before using a toothbrush and elbow grease to clean out the grunge. If the inside of the planter is still discolored after all this, wait a day or two and soak the piece in straight bleach such as Roman Cleanser™ or Clorox®. Do not do this if there is gold or silver trim! If all else fails, consider filling the planter with silk plants or flowers set into a base of florist foam. (See the next chapter for more on use and display.)

Figural planters and vases can be pretty, they can be cute, they can be funny. They are children of an older era and deserve to be collected. But — let's face it — the majority of them are not in the same category as, say, a thousand-dollar piece of art pottery. We can afford to *use* these whimsical little objects, not just look at them.

A parade of small animals across your windowsill will brighten any room. If plant tending is not your thing, fill the containers with florist's foam and insert your choice of small silk flowers or leaves. Instant garden! The arrangements will be small, so you can even pick the whole thing up and shake it to dust the plants. You can even place candle glue or hot wax drippings in the planter and place a small candle in the midst of your plants. Try arrangements of similar planters, such as small animals or birds, on a coffee table or place a group on the shelves of the popular wood or brass multiple plant stands that can be found in most department stores or garden centers.

If you have an available sunny kitchen windowsill, maybe you would like to grow some herbs in your planters. This would be a good use for planters with inside grunge that just will not come out! If you want pot protection, line your planter with aluminum foil, being careful not to punch any holes in it. About ½" of fine gravel (try uncolored aquarium gravel) on the bottom will help with drainage. A sandy commercial potting soil mix comes next. Herbs that are happy in pots include chives, parsley, spicy globe basil, marjoram and some thymes. Don't drown them—remember your planters are glazed and water does not get much chance to evaporate. Basil, chives, and parsley can be grown from seed right in the container. (Soak parsley seed in hot water overnight before sowing.) Or look for small plants at your local garden shop or perhaps even in your supermarket's produce section.

Children often enjoy planters in their rooms. A cactus of some type will generally do well in a planter, as will sansevieria, aloe, and jade plants, all of which are fairly child-proof, being of the "can't kill 'em with a club" type.

They will survive an occasional tumble to the floor and even get through the child's periodic enthusiasm for digging them up "to see if there are more roots."

If your planter is large enough, you can set an already-potted plant inside it, plastic or terra cotta pot and all. It will look more attractive if you hide the pot edges with strategically-placed sphagnum moss.

The little humped-back cat planters look authentic with a tall, fuzzy cactus plant placed to look like the cat's tail. Put a few tumble-polished stones on the soil surface to dress it up. Some of these cats originally had cigar-shaped felt "tails" that were treated to use as air fresheners. Remember Air-Wick™?

Thinking of new ways to use your planters will add a lot of interest to your collection. Another herb-related use would be filling them with a good potpourri mixture. This is especially nice for the larger, flat planters, such as the open-back ducks. If you have your own outdoor herb bed, you're way ahead of the game on this one. Otherwise, look in your local herb shop, farmers' market or craft shop for a good mixture. A little vial of essential oil in the fragrance of your choice will revive your potpourri mixture when the fragrance begins to fade. For extra interest, scatter small seashells, gold-sprayed tiny pine cones, or sweetgum balls on top of the mixture. You can even cheat a bit and add some tiny silk rosebuds. A small planter can be filled with an aromatic mixture of whole cloves, whole allspice, bay leaves, broken cinnamon sticks, etc. This can be harvested right in your grocery or bulk food shop. Add a little ground orris root to make the fragrance last even longer.

Deep planters or vases can be used on your desk or by the telephone to hold pens, pencils and letter openers. Or put a couple in the bathroom to hold cotton balls or bath beads. Some folks feel after awhile that their animal and bird planters are "friends." One collector we know put some of them on a wide windowsill that looks out into the backyard garden "so they can see the flowers," she says. Above all, have fun with your collection.

Left: Lovely lady in green dress and hat is marked Lady Margaret, A1875C. 8½" tall. $18.00 – 20.00. Right: Lady with parasol wearing rose/pink dress, 8¼" tall. Marked only A463. $18.00 – 20.00.

Left: Windblown blonde lady, 8" tall. Marked Made in Japan with black/silver keystone sticker. $18.00 – 20.00. Right: Lady in wine-colored dress with applied floral trim, 8¼" tall. Marked (c) George Z. Lefton 1957-164. $50.00 – 55.00.

Left: Stylized dancer, 8¼" tall. Marked only #234. $15.00 – 18.00. Right: Lady with hat, 7½" tall. Lefton sticker, Made in Japan #5658. $20.00 – 25.00.

Left: Demure coated girl 6" tall, marked Florence Ceramics, Pasadena, Calif. $45.00 – 50.00. Right: Lady with much gold trim, 6¼" tall. Unmarked. $20.00 – 25.00 mainly because of the gold and applied detailing.

Left: Brunette lady, 6¾" tall, marked Florence Ceramics. $50.00 – 55.00. Right: Blonde lady with green dress and hat, 6". Unmarked. $18.00 – 20.00.

Left: Little girl with hat and skirt up, 5½" tall. Doesn't she look startled? Unmarked. $12.00 – 14.00. Right: Brunette girl, 5¾" tall, with basket. Unmarked. $10.00 – 12.00.

Left: Girl carrying hat, 6¾" tall. Unmarked. $10.00 – 12.00. Right: Girl with bowl, 5¾" tall. Unmarked. $8.00 – 10.00.

Left: Girl with brown and rose-shaded dress, 6¼" tall. Marked RELPO #5878. $10.00 – 12.00. Right: Blonde girl with turquoise dress and armload of flowers, 7¼" tall. Marked (c) Samson Import Co. 1960. Also has RELPO sticker and Japan 4038. $12.00 – 15.00.

Left: Girl, 7¼" tall. Impressed RELPO 5940. $12.00 – 15.00. Right: Girl holding hat, 7¾" tall. Re-stamped Japan in horseshoe. $10.00 – 12.00.

Left: Brunette with basket of flowers, 6"
tall. Marked Lefton, Japan 3000/c.
$25.00 – 30.00. Right: Slender blonde
in white dress with gold trim, 6¾" tall.
Unmarked. $20.00 – 25.00.

Left: Valentine girl at mailbox, 5¾" tall.
Marked RELPO with black stamp and
A1136. $20.00 – 25.00. Right: Harvest-
time girl with sheaf of wheat, 5¾" tall.
Marked Matilda #1685A. $18.00 –
20.00.

Two little girls in rose-colored dresses
that may be the same mold but with different decorations applied, such as the
basket and the hat. Left: 7¼" tall; right:
7" tall. Unmarked. $18.00 – 20.00.

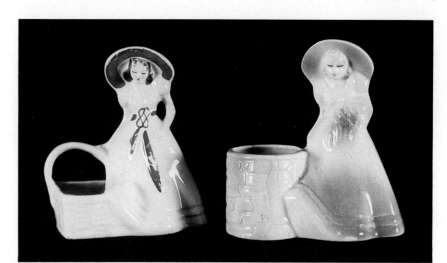

Left: Girl with basket, 5⅝" tall. Brush-McCoy. $25.00 – 30.00. Right: Girl at stone well, 5¾" tall. Unmarked. $10.00 – 12.00.

Lady Godiva on her horse, 7" long. Stamped Japan in black. $18.00 – 22.00.

Left: Girl with gold trim, 6½" tall. Unmarked. $15.00 – 20.00. Right: Girl with parasol, 7½" tall. Unmarked. $18.00 – 22.00.

Lovely pair of figural vases. Left: Gentleman, 7¼" tall. Japan. $18.00 – 22.00. Right: Lady, 7" tall. Japan. $18.00 – 22.00.

Left: Blonde with bowl, 5¾" tall. Unmarked. $8.00 – 10.00. Right: Little girl with basket, 6½" tall. Shawnee. $12.00 – 14.00.

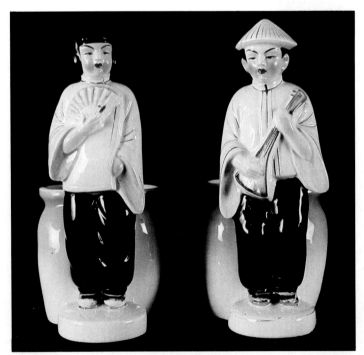

Left: Oriental girl with fan, 9" tall. Right. Oriental man, 9¼" tall. Unmarked. $10.00 – 12.00 each.

Left: Oriental lady, 6" tall. Souvenir piece of Van Wert, Ohio. Japan. $8.00 – 12.00. Right: Oriental boy, 5" tall. Marked Pat. Pending, Joan Lea Creations, Hand painted, USA. $8.00 – 10.00.

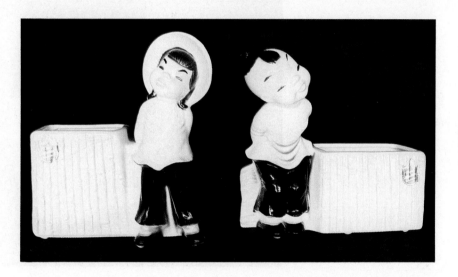

Oriental girl and boy with bamboo planters. Girl is 7" x 8" tall; boy is 7½" x 7¾" long. Unmarked. $10.00 – 12.00 each.

Left: Oriental couple, 3¾" tall, marked USA 573. Shawnee. $12.00 – 14.00. Right: Standing Oriental girl. Should have chains from her shoulder yoke through the buckets. 6¼" tall. Unmarked. $8.00 – 12.00 with chains.

Pair of Oriental shelf-sitters, 7" from head to foot. Unmarked. $8.00 – 10.00 each.

Oriental girl with pot, 5½" tall. Royal Copley.
$10.00 – 12.00.

Left: Pink oriental boy kneeling, 9" tall. Marked only with #7. $8.00 – 12.00. Right: Chinese girl with big hat, 7½" tall. Royal Copley. $25.00 – 28.00.

Two cute Oriental kids, 4" x 4½". Carry NAPCO, Japan sticker. $10.00 – 12.00 each.

Left: Oriental man with "honey cart", 5" tall, introduced 1950. McCoy. $10.00 – 12.00. Right: Couple with tub, 7¾" long. Unmarked. $8.00 – 10.00.

Left: Cherub, 5" tall, marked Made in Japan. $8.00 – 10.00. Right: Buddha, 6½" tall. Shawnee, USA. $22.00 – 24.00.

Left: White angel with gold, 7" tall. Stanfordware. $18.00 – 20.00. Right: Baby on globe, 7½" tall. Unmarked. $12.00 – 15.00.

White cherubs with basket, 7½" long. Unmarked. $12.00 – 14.00.

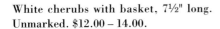

Cherub with rabbit and egg, 4¾", tall. bisque. Marked C. $8.00 – 10.00.

Girl leaning on barrel, 6¼" tall. Royal Copley.
$15.00 – 17.00.

Left: Boy at tree stump, 6½" tall. USA Shawnee, 533. $10.00 – 12.00. Right: Boy at wall, 5⅜" tall. Stamped Made in Japan in red. $8.00 – 10.00.

Left: Boy, 5½" tall. Unmarked. $8.00 – 10.00. Right: Girl, 5¼" tall. Unmarked. $8.00 – 10.00.

Left: Dutch Girl 4⅝" tall, watering tulip by tub. Shawnee. $10.00 – 12.00. Center: Oriental man with basket, 4⅝" tall. McCoy. Introduced in 1949. $10.00 – 12.00. Right: Little girl at well. 5½" tall. Unmarked. $8.00 – 10.00.

Left and Center: Boy and girl at gate, 4¼" tall. USA 581, Shawnee. $12.00 – 14.00 each. Right: Oriental girl, 3½" tall. USA 547, Shawnee. $14.00 – 16.00.

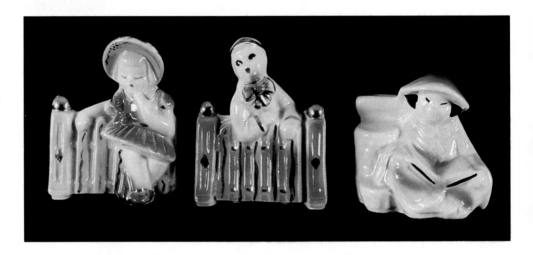

Left: Couple "Dancing Cheek to Cheek," 5¼" tall. Unmarked. $6.00 – 8.00. Right: Couple, 7⅜" tall. Unmarked. $8.00 – 10.00.

Left: Humpty Dumpty, 4½" tall. McCoy. $12.00 – 15.00. Right: Jack and Jill, 4⅝" tall. Unmarked. $8.00 – 10.00.

Left: Angel, 6" tall. Also made for use as a wall pocket. Unmarked. $8.00 – 10.00. Right: Whistle player with gold line trim, 5¼" tall. Unmarked. $12.00 – 15.00.

Left: Kewpie at stump, 5½" tall. Unmarked, probably Haeger. $6.00 – 8.00. Right: Little girl, 5¼" tall. Haeger. $7.00 – 9.00.

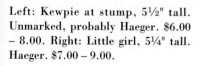

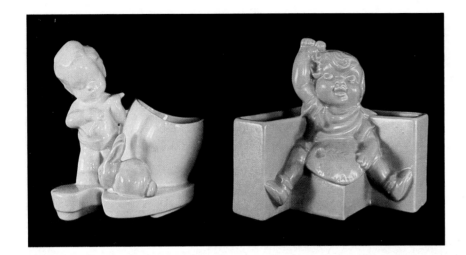

Left: Baby hunter with pink bunny, 6⅜" tall. Unmarked. $7.00 – 9.00. Right: Little Jack Horner, 6¾" tall. Haeger. $8.00 – 10.00.

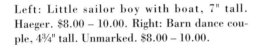

Left: Little sailor boy with boat, 7" tall. Haeger. $8.00 – 10.00. Right: Barn dance couple, 4¾" tall. Unmarked. $8.00 – 10.00.

Left: Pair of children, 7⅜" tall. Unmarked. $8.00 – 10.00. Right: Drummer girl, 6¾" tall. Unmarked. $9.00 – 12.00.

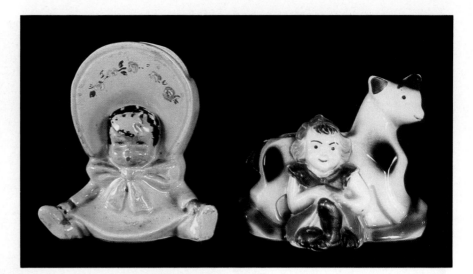

Left: Baby with hood, 6⅛" tall. USA #219 Brush. $15.00 – 20.00. Right: Girl with cow, 5⅛" tall. Brush. $15.00 – 20.00.

Left: Blue Madonna, 6½" tall. Royal Windsor. $18.00 – 22.00. Right: White Madonna and child. 5¾" tall. INARCO 1963. Cleveland, Ohio, E-322. $10.00 – 12.00.

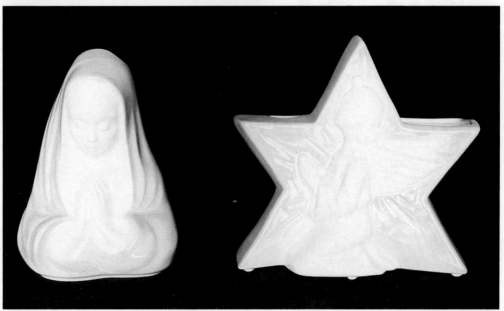

Left: Different shade of blue Madonna, 6½" tall. Royal Windsor. $18.00 – 20.00. Right: Star and angel, 6¾" tall. Made as candle or planter. Royal Copley. $15.00 – 20.00.

Madonna with lilies, 5¼" tall. Unmarked. $8.00 – 10.00.

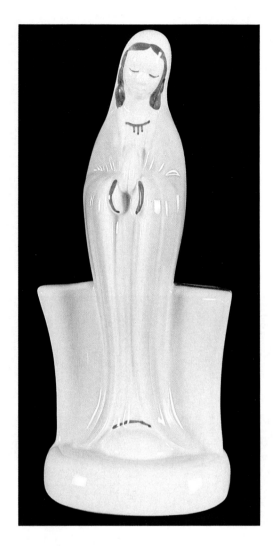

Madonna in blue robe, 12" tall. Unmarked. $12.00 – 15.00.

Angel in pink robe with gold trim, 10½" tall. Unmarked. $20.00 – 22.00.

Left: Head vase, 7" tall. Marked only USA. $25.00 – 30.00. Right: Praying Madonna, 7¾". Unmarked. $10.00 – 12.00.

Left: St. Francis, 12" tall. Marked INARCO, Japan. $12.00 – 15.00. Right: Uncle Sam, 7½" tall. McCoy. $15.00 – 20.00.

Left: Girl with gold trim, 6¼" tall. Stanfordware. $8.00 – 12.00. Right: Boy at stump, 6½" tall. Stanfordware. $8.00 – 10.00.

Left: Little lady elf, 6" x 6½". Unmarked. $8.00 – 10.00. Right: Colonial couple, 5¾" tall. Unmarked. $7.00 – 9.00.

Left: Pushcart man, 5⅞" tall, American Bisque. $12.00 – 14.00. Right: Boy and girl, 7½" tall. Unmarked. $8.00 – 10.00.

Left: Little girl feeding duck, 4½" tall. Unmarked. $7.00 – 9.00. Center: Children in shoe, 3⅞" tall. Czechoslovakian. $10.00 – 12.00. Right: Golfer, 6¼" tall. Unmarked. $10.00 – 12.00.

Left: Mexican man at tree vase, 5½" tall. Red stamped Japan. $7.00 – 9.00. Right: Aladdin's girl friend 5⅞" tall, with gold trim. Unmarked. $10.00 – 12.00.

Left: Accordion man, 3¾" tall. Unmarked. $7.00 – 9.00. Right: Pushcart man, 6¾" tall. American Bisque. $12.00 – 14.00.

Left: Baby ballerina, 5½" tall, Haeger. $8.00 – 10.00. Right: Baby cooking, 5½" tall, Haeger. $8.00 – 10.00.

Left: Side show man with horn, 4¾" tall. Unmarked. $9.00 – 12.00. Right: Humpty Dumpty, 5¾" tall. Unmarked. $12.00 – 14.00.

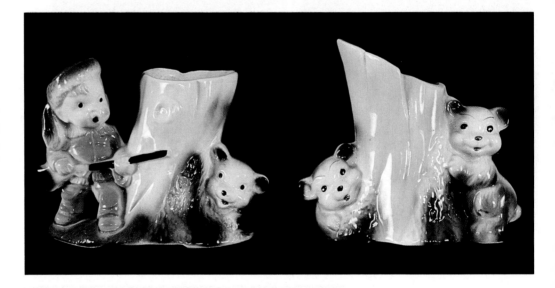

Left: Little Davy Crockett, 5" tall. American Bisque. $45.00 – 50.00. Right: Bears at tree, 5½" tall. American Bisque. $12.00 – 14.00.

Left: Mammy on scoop, 7" long. McCoy. $25.00 – 30.00. Right: Man on rolling pin, 7". McCoy. $25.00 – 30.00. These two are elusive. Introduced in 1953.

Left: Dutch girl with buckets, 6¼" tall. Unmarked. $9.00 – 12.00. Right: Seated girl with gold trim, 5¾" tall. Marked USA 616 Shawnee. $30.00 – 35.00.

Dutch couple with wishing well, 8½" long. Shawnee. $25.00 – 30.00.

Left: Elf on stump, 5⅛" tall. Unmarked. $7.00 – 9.00. Right: Dutch boy with tub, 6¼" tall. Royal Copley. $20.00 – 24.00.

Left: Dutch boy on wall, 6" x 6½".
Unmarked. $10.00 – 12.00.
Right: Dutch girl with shoe. 5⅛"
tall. Coventry Ware. $12.00 –
15.00.

Left: Dutch boy, 9¾" tall.
Unmarked. $10.00 – 12.00.
Right: Dutch girl with tulips,
7½" tall. USA, American
Bisque. $15.00 – 18.00.

Left: Dutch boy with buckets, 4"
tall. Black stamped Made in
Japan. $7.00 – 9.00. Right: Elf
with barrow, 3¾" tall. Shawnee.
$12.00 – 15.00.

Left: Child with cap, knees up. 5½" tall, real yarn hair. Unmarked. $15.00 – 20.00. Right: Man with hotdog wagon, 6" x 7". No mark. Very detailed mold. $18.00 – 20.00.

Golf caddy vase or planter, 8" tall. Isn't he cute? Unmarked. $8.00 – 10.00.

Left: Long-necked lady, 7" tall. Marked Kindell (c). $35.00 – 40.00. Right: Black with pot on shoulder, 5¾" tall. Gold trim. Marked Pat. Pending, Joan.....(unreadable). $18.00 – 20.00.

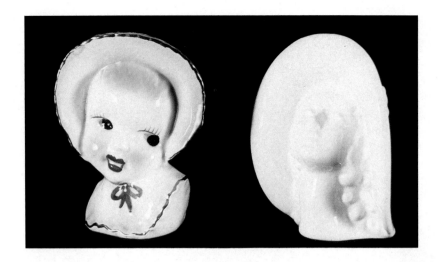

Left: Baby head, 5½" tall. Marked Shafer 24K Gold. $25.00 – 30.00. Right: White lady head, 5½". Marked only USA. $17.00 – 22.00.

Clown with drum, 5½" tall. Unmarked. $10.00 – 12.00.

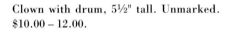

Clown with vase, 8¼" tall. Unmarked. $15.00 – 20.00.

Left: White clown, 5" tall. Unmarked. $9.00 – 12.00. Right: Clown flower pot holder, 4¾" tall. Shawnee. $18.00 – 22.00.

Left: Santa with bag, 5½" tall. Unmarked. $18.00 – 20.00. Right: Clown with drum, 6" tall. Unmarked. $7.00 – 9.00.

Left: Santa with railroad engine, 5⅜" x 6¾". Unmarked. $12.00 – 15.00. Right: Little girl, 4½" tall. Japan. $7.00 – 9.00.

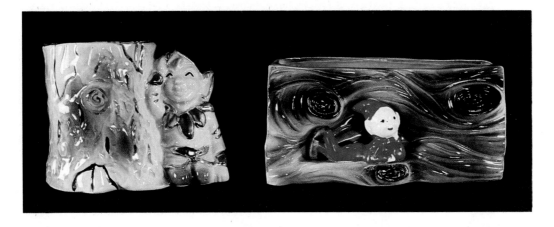

Left: Elf at stump, 3⅜", gold trim. Unmarked. $10.00 – 12.00. Right: Elf on log, 6¼" long. Unmarked. $8.00 – 10.00.

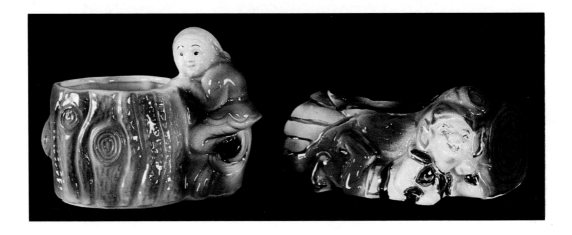

Left: Elf leaning on stump, 4½". Unmarked. $9.00 – 12.00. Right: Reclining elf with log, 7" long. American Bisque. $9.00 – 12.00.

Left: Elf riding swan, 5" x 6". Unmarked, possibly Brush. $10.00 – 12.00. Center: Sprite climbing into pot, 3½". Marked USA 536. $6.00 – 8.00. Right: Elf with barrow, 5" long. Shawnee. $12.00 – 15.00.

Left: Elves with log, 8" long.
McCoy. $12.00 – 15.00. Right:
Wee man with bucket, 6".
Unmarked. $8.00 – 10.00.

Left: Red elf with chest, 4¾"
long. Marked Gilner. $7.00 –
9.00. Right: Yellow elf on shoe,
6" long. Unmarked. $7.00 –
9.00.

Balinese girl, 8¼" tall. Royal Copley.
$25.00 – 30.00.

Colonial old woman, 8" tall. Royal Copley. $35.00 – 40.00.

Blackamoor, 8½" tall. Royal Copley. $50.00 – 55.00.

Colonial old man, 8" tall. Royal Copley. $35.00 – 40.00.

Left: Knight on horseback, 8".
Hull Pottery. $75.00 – 80.00.
Right: Fox hunter, 8¾" long.
Unmarked. $25.00 – 30.00.

Steeplechaser, 12" long. Unmarked.
$25.00 – 30.00.

Banana boat from McCoy Pottery
Calypso line introduced about 1955.
This also introduced a new method
of decorating which gave a mottled
or speckled effect. $35.00 – 40.00

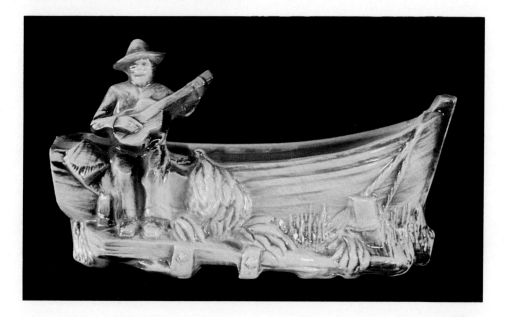

Left: Man with guitar, 7½" x 4⅞". Also McCoy Calypso line. $25.00 – 35.00. Right: Couple at well, 5¾" tall. Unmarked. $8.00 – 12.00.

Plow boy, 8¼" long. McCoy Pottery introduced about 1955. $22.00 – 25.00.

Village smithy, 7½" long. Legend is "Under The Spreading Chestnut Tree." McCoy Pottery. $20.00 – 25.00. Introduced 1953.

Rodeo cowboy roping steer, 7¾" long. McCoy
Pottery about 1955. $25.00 – 30.00.

Wild West rodeo cowboy, 7½" long. McCoy
Pottery introduced around 1955. $25.00 –
30.00.

Country peddler, 8¾" long. Unmarked.
Lovely detail. $18.00 – 20.00.

Covered wagon with team and driver, 10" long. Very detailed. Unmarked except for #02341. $18.00 – 22.00.

Hunter with dog, 11½" long. Brush Pottery. $25.00 – 30.00.

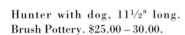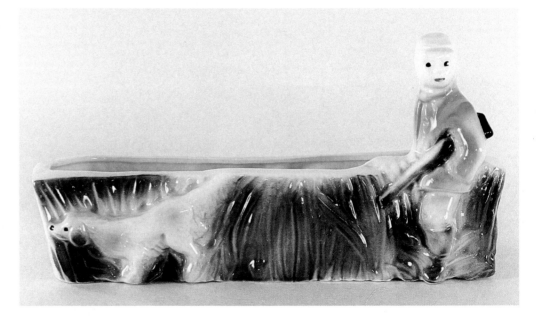

Left: Bird on fence vase, 3¾". Japan. $6.00 – 8.00. Right: Girl feeding duck vase, 5¾" tall. Unmarked import. $8.00 – 12.00.

Left: Girl in plaid dress, 4½".
Unmarked. $12.00 – 14.00. Center: Girl
with hat, 4½". Stamped Made in Japan
with wreath and plum blossom. $14.00 –
18.00. Right: Blonde girl, 5" tall, sticker
reads Norcrest Fine China, Japan.
$15.00 – 20.00.

Left: Girl with yellow dress, 4½".
Unmarked. $15.00 – 20.00. Cen-
ter: Brunette with locket, 4½".
Marked deLee Art, California.
$15.00 – 20.00. Right: Bare shoul-
der lady, 6". Royal Copley. $25.00
– 30.00.

Left: Girl holding skirt, 5". Unmarked.
$8.00 – 10.00. Right: Girl with hat, 5¼".
Unmarked. $8.00 – 10.00.

Left: Girl in black, 6" tall. Umbrella missing. Made in Japan, UCAGO. $10.00 – 12.00. Right: Rose-dressed brunette, 6⅛" tall. Unmarked. $10.00 – 12.00.

Left: Seated girl, 5½" tall. Marked Florence Ceramics. $25.00 – 30.00. Right: Oriental boy, 5" tall. RELPO K1610. $9.00 – 12.00.

The Daisy Sisters, 6½" tall. RELPO 6081. $9.00 – 12.00 each.

Left: Girl in green, 6" tall. Unmarked. $9.00 – 12.00. Right: Girl with birdbath, 6" tall. Unmarked. $9.00 – 12.00.

Left: Girl with hat in hand, 8". Lefton stamp. $12.00 – 15.00. Right: Blonde with blue dress, 6¾". Samson Import Co., 1962, Japan. $9.00 – 12.00.

Left: Angel with halfmoon, 4¼" tall. "Your Lucky Star Guardian Angel" NAPCO. $8.00 – 10.00. Center: Pink lady, 5". Marked TV-1361. $7.00 – 9.00. Right: Christmas girl, 5¼" tall. NAPCO 1956, AX1690PA. $9.00 – 12.00.

Left: This 8¼" tall girl with the ruffled skirt is missing most of an arm, but she was so pretty, we had to show her anyway! Unmarked. $10.00 – 12.00, in perfect condition. Right: Little girl, 5½". Unmarked. $6.00 – 8.00.

Left: Christmas girl with packages, 7" tall. Marked Fine Ceramics Hand Painted, Japan. Also has NAPCO sticker by Gift Craft. $20.00 – 25.00. Right: Christmas girl in red, 7". RELPO A1964. $18.00 – 20.00.

Left: French couple, 6⅛". Marked Made in Japan with black stamp and also impressed. $15.00 – 18.00. Right: Christmas girl with candy cane, 4½" tall. RELPO Sticker, Japan. $12.00 – 15.00.

Left: Valentine girl, 6" x 6". Lefton China. $20.00 – 25.00. Right: Christmas girl with package, 4⅝" x 5". Marked S715B Lefton. $20.00 – 25.00.

Valentine girls. Left: 6¾" tall, RELPO A918. $18.00 – 20.00. Right: 7⅜" tall. Marked only CR142. $18.00 – 20.00.

Valentine girls. Left: 5½" tall, Napcoware, Made in Japan. $18.00 – 20.00. Right: 5¾" tall, Made in Japan. $18.00 – 20.00.

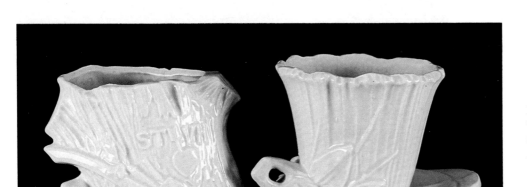

Left: Stump with lover's initials "S.T. loves V.H.", 4". Unmarked. $8.00 – 10.00. Right: Lotus leaf and flower, 4¾". McCoy. $9.00 – 12.00.

Left: Gourd or squash, 2⅞" x 5¼". Marked Paradise Products, Inc. 1970 (c). $5.00 – 7.00. Right: Mushrooms and tree stump, 4½" tall. American Bisque. $12.00 – 14.00.

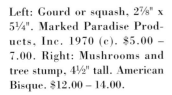

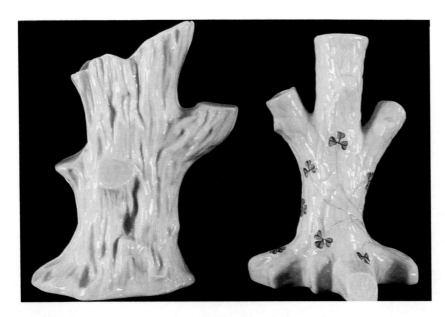

Left: Tree trunk, 6½" tall. Irish Beleek green mark. $150.00 – 160.00. Right: Tree trunk with shamrocks, 6". Irish Beleek green mark. $150.00 – 160.00.

Left: Wheeled golf bag, 7" tall. Unmarked. $9.00 – 12.00. Right: Wheelbarrow, 4½" tall, Shawnee USA. $20.00 – 25.00.

Left: Pipe, 4½" x 8½". Unmarked. $8.00 – 10.00. Right: Bell, 4¾". Allover gold. These come in a set of graduated sizes. Unmarked. $10.00 – 12.00.

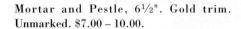

Mortar and Pestle, 6½". Gold trim. Unmarked. $7.00 – 10.00.

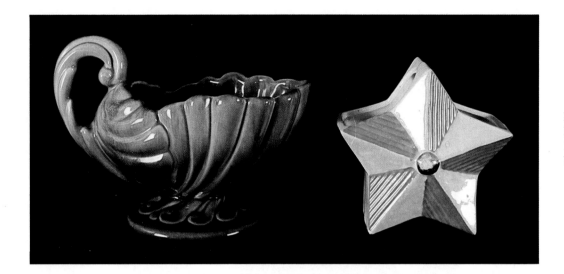

Left: Shell on foot, 7¾" long. Haeger Pottery. $10.00 – 12.00. Right: Star, 4¾". Unmarked. $7.00 – 9.00.

Left: Hand vase, 8⅝". McCoy. $8.00 – 12.00. Right: Sprinkling can, 5½" tall. Can be used as such. Shawnee USA. $16.00 – 18.00.

Left: Cornucopia, 3¼". Unmarked. $5.00 – 7.00. Center: Blue pitcher with flowers, 3⅝" tall. McCoy. $7.00 – 9.00. Right: Cornucopia, 4". Unmarked. $5.00 – 7.00.

Left: Coal scuttle, 6½" long. Unmarked. $7.00 – 9.00. Center: Hand vase, 6¾". Shawnee. $12.00 – 14.00. Right: Cornucopia, 4¾". Shawnee USA #835. $12.00 – 14.00.

Left: Hand vase with applied flowers, 5½". Black stamped Made in Japan. $8.00 – 10.00. Right: Hand bud vase, 6". Cash Family Clinchfield Artware Pottery, Hand Painted, Erwin, Tennessee. $8.00 – 12.00.

Watering can, 10½" long, can be used as such. Marked A Tele-gift (c) 1985, Made in Korea. $6.00 – 9.00.

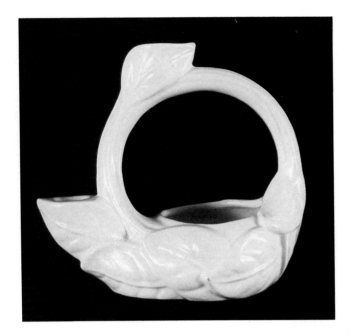

Leafy candle/planter, 7¼" x 8¼".
Unmarked. $7.00 – 9.00.

Left: Pair of hands with vase, 5½".
Applied flowers and gold line trim.
Marked Bone China Flowers. $6.00 –
8.00. Right: Lacy basket, 6½" long.
Impressed "Italy." $7.00 – 9.00.

Left: Japanese lantern, 7".
Unmarked. $6.00 – 8.00. Right:
White coach with applied flow-
ers and gold line trim, 4½"
Unmarked. $6.00 – 8.00.

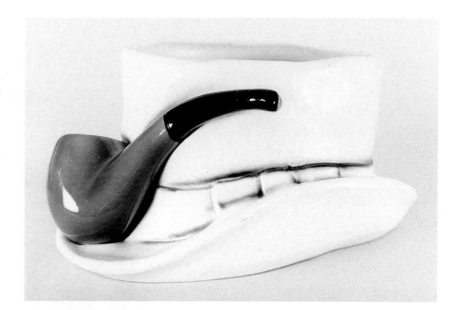

Hat with pipe, 3¾" x 7½". Marked Lefton, Japan, #H5959. $15.00 – 20.00.

Left: Some of the children from The Old
Woman in The Shoe, along with their
home, 5" tall. Shawnee, USA. $18.00 –
20.00. Right: Phonograph, 7¼" tall.
Unmarked. $12.00 – 15.00.

Left: Boxing gloves, 5½". Introduced
by McCoy about 1959. $18.00 –
20.00. Right: Baseball glove, 6". Also
by McCoy. $18.00 – 20.00.

Left: Oak leaves with acorns, 7¼"
long. Unmarked. $10.00 – 12.00.
Right: Peanut, 7½" long. Brush
USA. $15.00 – 20.00.

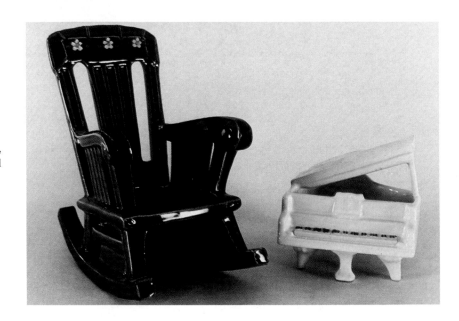

Left: Rocking chair, 8¾" tall. McCoy, USA,
introduced 1954. $18.00 – 22.00. Right: Grand
piano, 6" long. McCoy USA. $15.00 – 18.00.

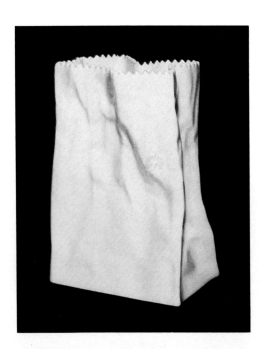

Paper bag, 6" tall. Marked Rosenthal Studio
Linie, Rosenthal. $8.00 – 10.00.

Pump with oaken bucket, 5¼" x 5¼". INARCO.
$9.00 – 12.00.

Sleigh with holly, 8" long. Unmarked. $10.00 – 12.00.

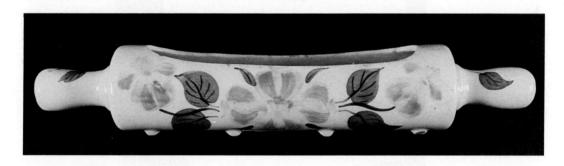

Rolling pin with hand painted flowers, 14" long. Product of the Cash Family, Clinchfield Artware Pottery about 1945. This was one of the first molds Cash used. The clay was mixed in their washing machine, and the product fired in the oven. Then Mrs. Cash took to the road to sell it! $10.00 – 12.00.

Left: Heart with applied flowers, 5¼" tall. "To Mother". Marked only #1816. $9.00 – 12.00. Right: Open book with applied flowers, 6" tall. Pearlized finish. Made in China currently. $5.00 – 7.00.

Open book with kitchen prayer, 6¼" long. Unmarked. $7.00 – 9.00.

Left: Open book, "Thinking of You", 4¾" x 6¼". Unmarked. $10.00 – 12.00. Right: Picture frame, 4" x 4¾", with Lord's Prayer. $6.00 – 9.00.

Left: Open book. "To Mother With Love", 4¾" x 6". Unmarked. $10.00 – 12.00. Right: Open book with Lord's Prayer, 5" x 6½". Royal Windsor. $10.00 – 12.00.

Left: Open book, "Happy Anniversary", 5" x 6½". Right: "Happy Birthday." Both marked Books of Remembrance by Royal Windsor, Design Patented, in gold. $10.00 – 12.00 each.

Log house, evidently for some sort of wee forest people, 12¼" long. Unmarked. $15.00 – 18.00.

Fireplace, combination planter and lamp, 8¼" x 10" long. Originally had red plastic sheet fit into opening to resemble fire. McCoy. $40.00 – 45.00.

Liberty Bell planter, 8½" x 9¾". McCoy USA. The story is that the designer of this piece was English and he found information that stated the ringing of the bell was July 8, 1776. So, that is the date he put on the piece, 8 July 1776! Later the date was corrected to read 4 July 1776. The legend on the back of the piece is "And a Nation is born." $50.00 – 60.00. Introduced about 1954.

Left: Wishing well, legend "Wishing You Well" around the rim of the well, 8". Marked only USA #200. $9.00 – 12.00. Right: Wishing well, 4½". Unmarked. $7.00 – 9.00.

Fisherman, legend says "Down by the old mill stream". 7¾" long. Introduced about 1953 by McCoy. $20.00 – 25.00.

Row house, with dried flower bouquet, 7¼"
tall . Unmarked. Probably Japan. $10.00 –
12.00.

Old mill, 5¾" x 7". Shawnee #767. $28.00 –
30.00.

House and garden, 11¾" long. Brush Pottery. $40.00 – 45.00.

House with stone fence and gate, 11" long. Brush #887. $40.00 – 45.00.

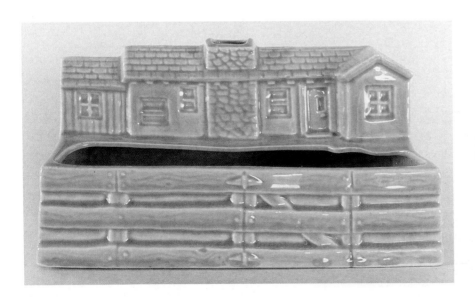

House with board fence, 11" long. Brush #888. $40.00 – 45.00.

Left: Bassinet with flowers and drape, 9" long. McCoy Pottery. $12.00 – 15.00. Right: Ruffled bassinet, says "Congratulations" on the ribbon, 7½" long. Stanford Pottery. $10.00 – 12.00.

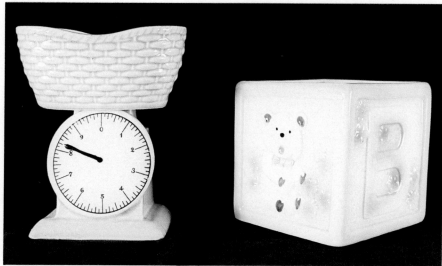

Left: Baby scale, 6½". Made in Japan. $9.00 – 12.00. Right: Baby block, 4¾". Marked "Giftwares Co., Inc. Nancy Pew. Taiwan." $6.00 – 8.00.

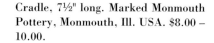

Cradle, 7½" long. Marked Monmouth Pottery, Monmouth, Ill. USA. $8.00 – 10.00.

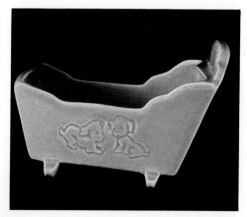

Left: Baby buggy, 7½" long. Unmarked. $7.00 – 10.00. Right: Bassinet, 3¼" x 5". Unmarked. $5.00 – 7.00.

Gondola, 11¼" long. McCoy Pottery. Some versions have oarlocks on one side, some do not. Introduced about 1955. $18.00 – 22.00.

Left: Davy Crockett canoe, 8½" long. American Bisque. $55.00 – 60.00. Right: Natchez showboat, 10" long. Brush Pottery. $25.00 – 30.00.

Left: Another Natchez side-wheeler, 10¾" long. American Bisque. $15.00 – 20.00. Right: Paddleboat "Lorena", 8¾". This boat is an operating stern-wheeler on the Muskingum River from Zanesville, Ohio. Marked "Bi-Centennial Project of Zanesville Area Chamber of Commerce, 1976." McCoy, USA. $20.00 – 25.00.

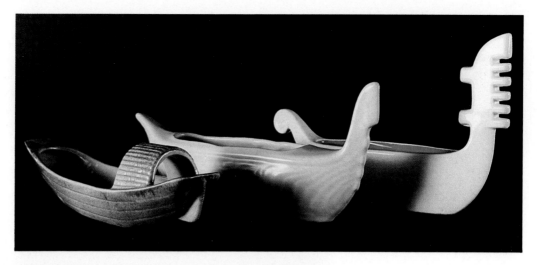

Left: Asian-style boat, 10" long. Gonder, USA #550. $12.00 – 15.00. Center: Viking-style, 12" long. Shawnee USA. $15.00 – 18.00. Right: Viking-style, 10½" long. Made in Czechoslovakia. #7952. $25.00 – 30.00.

Left: Sailboat, 7" tall. Made in Japan. $8.00 – 10.00. Right: Star, 5". Royal Copley. This comes with planter cavity on one side and candlestick on other. $7.00 – 9.00.

Tugboat, 9½" long. American Bisque. $22.00 – 25.00.

Left: Railroad engine, 5" with 4½" gondola. McCoy Ltd., USA. $18.00 – 20.00. Right: Cable car, 6½" long. Unmarked. $15.00 – 20.00.

Left: Railroad engine, 10" long. Unmarked. $15.00 – 20.00. Right: Black engine with gold trim, 9". Stanford Pottery. $15.00 – 20.00.

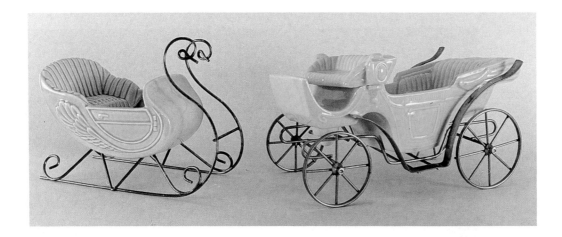

Left: Cutter on brass runners, 6¾" long. Metlox Pottery Nostalgia Line. $75.00 – 80.00. Right: Victoria, 10¾" long. Also Metlox Nostalgia Line. $75.00 – 80.00. This line was Evan Shaw's favorite Artware line. Each item was created as realistically as possible. Shaw created the designs himself. It was produced from the 1940s through the 1960s. Figures of horses and people were created to go with the transportation pieces. These accessory pieces are difficult to find.

Stagecoach for U.S. Mail, 11½" long.
Marked (c) 1952 Lane & Co. They were
probably a jobber, as we're sure the
piece was produced by Metlox. $70.00 –
80.00.

Left: Runabout, 10" long.
McCoy Pottery. $15.00 –
18.00. Right: "Smooshed"
auto with gold trim, 3½".
This one must have been in
an   awful   accident!
Unmarked. $12.00 – 15.00.

Left: 1930s coupe with even
the underside detailed, 7"
long. Unmarked. $12.00 –
15.00. Right: 1954 Chevrolet
Corvette convertible, 9½"
long. Marked GOLDOR.
$12.00 – 15.00.

Left: Auto with right hand control, 6". Unmarked. $10.00 – 12.00. Right: Morgan 44 auto, 8". Marked Floraline USA. McCoy Pottery, LCC 532. $12.00 – 14.00.

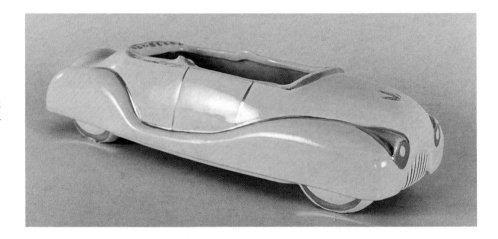

Stylized convertible, Shafer gold trim, 12" long. Brush USA. $35.00 – 40.00.

Concord coach, 10" long. Marked (c) Allen-Shaw. Metlox. $90.00 – 100.00.

Left: Covered wagon, 7". Unmarked. $12.00 – 15.00. Right: Wagon, 5" long. Marked Zane's Trace – 1982 Commemoration. $15.00. – 20.00.

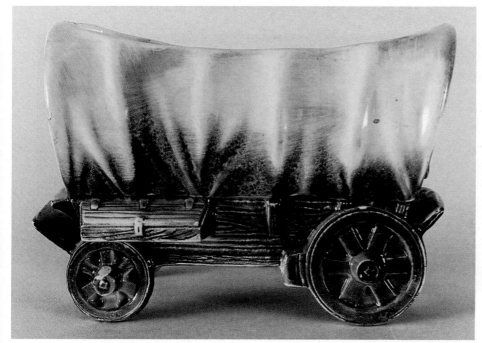

Covered wagon, 10¾" long. Shawnee #733. $35.00 – 40.00.

Wagon wheel, 8¼" tall. McCoy Pottery. This will be found in various colors as a planter, lamp or vase. $20.00 – 25.00.

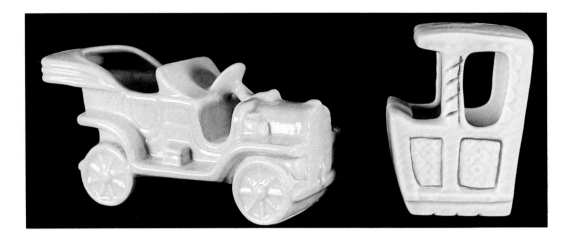

Left: Auto, 6¾" long. Unmarked. $8.00 – 10.00. Right: Part of a sedan chair, 4" tall. Unmarked. $7.00 – 9.00.

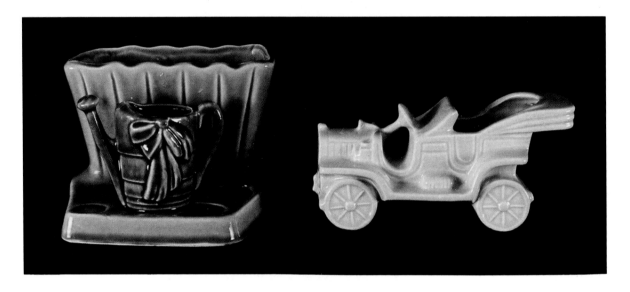

Left: Watering can with pot, 4" x 5¾". R.R.P. Roseville, Ohio #1302. This is Robinson-Ransbottom Co. Pottery. $10.00 – 12.00. Right: Another color variation of the auto shown above. $8.00 – 10.00.

Covered wagon, 9½" x 6½". Unmarked. $12.00 – 15.00.

Fire engine, 7½" x 6" long. American
Bisque. $25.00 – 30.00.

Cable car, 6¾" long. American Bisque.
$25.00 – 30.00.

Left: Silver shoe, 5½" long. $7.00 –
9.00. Right: Color variation of same
shoe. Stanford Ware. $5.00 – 7.00.

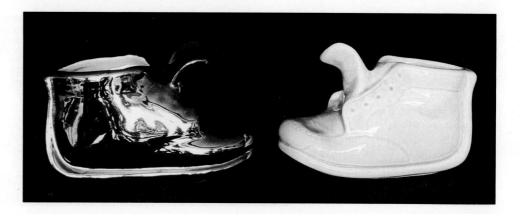

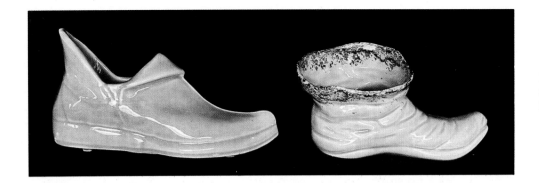

Left: Boot, 8½" long. Unmarked. $5.00 – 7.00. Right: Bootie, 6½" long. Unmarked. $6.00 – 8.00.

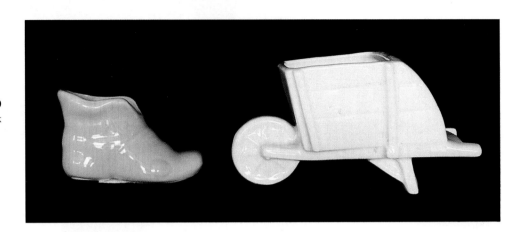

Left: Bootie, 4" long. Unmarked. $5.00 – 7.00. Right: Wheelbarrow, 3½" x 6¼". Shawnee. $8.00 – 10.00.

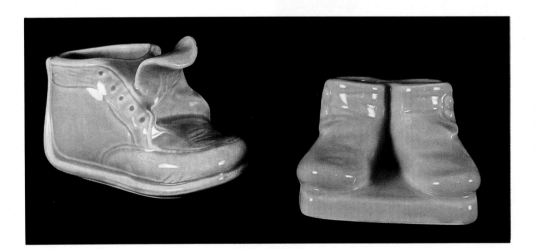

Left: Baby shoe, 5½". Color variation of Stanford #967. $5.00 – 7.00. Right: Baby shoes, 4" wide. Shawnee USA. $10.00 – 12.00.

Left: Lustre baby shoe with gold laces, 2" x 4". Unmarked. $6.00 – 8.00. Center: Pair button baby shoes, 2½" x 3". Shawnee Pottery. These came in pairs and in other colors and sizes. $10.00 – 12.00 pair. Right: Baby shoe with buttons, 2⅜" x 3⅞". A little different than the Shawnee. Unmarked. $5.00 – 7.00 each.

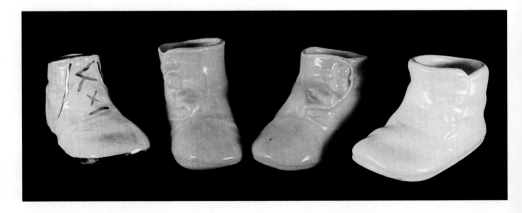

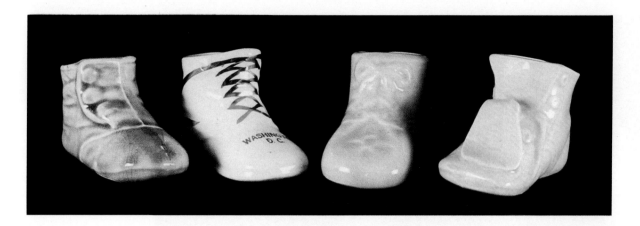

Left: Three-button baby shoe, 2⅝". Unmarked. $5.00 – 7.00. Next: Shoe with 22K gold laces, 2¾". Souvenir of Washington, D.C. Brush USA label. $25.00 – 30.00 pair. Next: Collar foot shoe, 2¾". Shawnee. $6.00 – 8.00. Right: Tongue-out shoe, 2¾". Color variation of previously shown Stanford Ware shoe. $5.00 – 7.00.

Left: Engineer's boot, 4½" tall. Shawnee USA. $10.00 – 12.00. Right: Joined baby shoes, 3½" x 6". Haeger Pottery. $7.00 – 9.00.

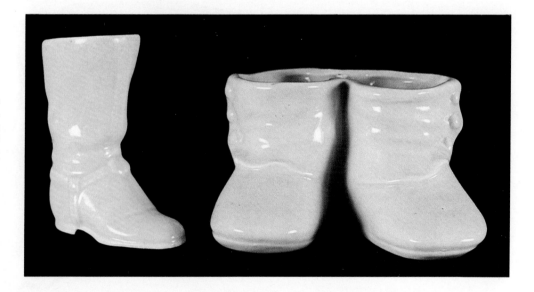

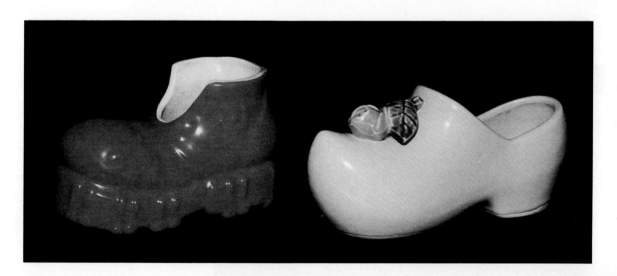

Left: Sports shoe, 6" long. Consensus of opinion on this one is McCoy. $8.00 – 12.00. Right: Dutch shoe with flower, 7½" long. McCoy. $8.00 – 10.00. Introduced about 1948.

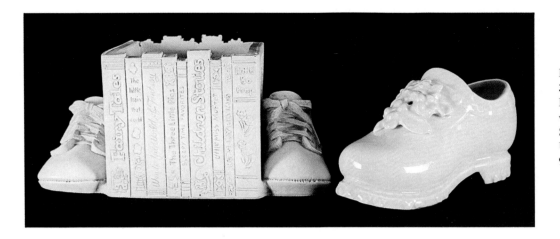

Left: Baby shoe-bookend piece, 3¾" x 8". Resin material. Marked Made for FTD, 1982 with logo. $5.00 – 7.00. Right: Sports shoe, 6⅜" long. Marked U.S. Zone, Germany. $6.00 – 9.00.

Ski boot, 4" tall. Sticker reads PARMA by AAI. Made in Japan. $10.00 – 12.00.

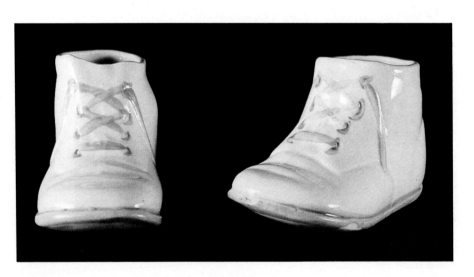

Baby shoes with laces, 3¼". Unmarked. $10.00 – 12.00 pair.

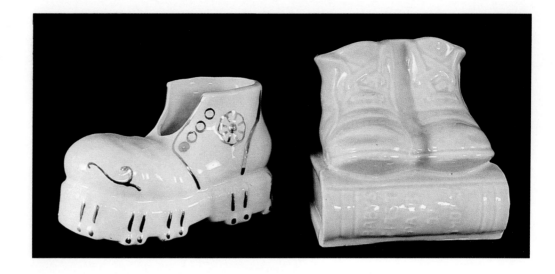

Left: Athletic shoe, 6". Color variation of the red one presumed to be unmarked McCoy. This has gold trim. $10.00 – 12.00. Right: Pair of baby shoes on book, 4⅝" tall. Book's spine says "Baby's First Pair of Shoes." Unmarked. $10.00 – 12.00.

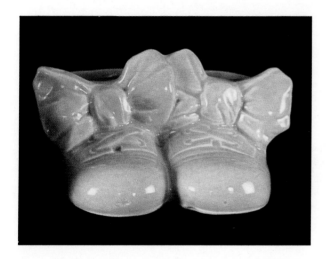

Bow-trimmed baby shoe pair, 5½" wide. McCoy Pottery. Introduced 1948. $10.00 – 14.00.

Left: Bowling ball and pins, 5⅜" tall. Unmarked. $10.00 – 12.00. Right: Dutch shoe, 5" long. Label reads Caliente Potterys, Registered California. Impressed is 316 CA. $8.00 – 10.00.

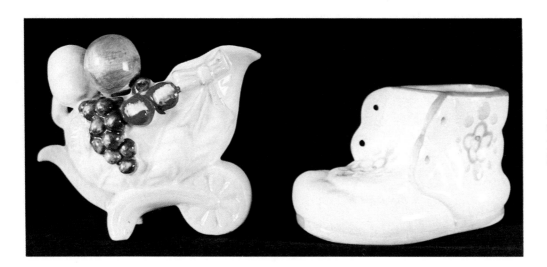

Left: Barrow with fruit, 5½" long. UCAGO Japan. $6.00 – 9.00. Right: Decorated baby shoe, 5¾" long. Unmarked. $5.00 – 7.00.

Left: Shoe with laces, 4¾" long. Unmarked. $7.00 – 9.00. Right: Alarm clock, 4⅜" tall. Shawnee USA 1262. $12.00 – 15.00.

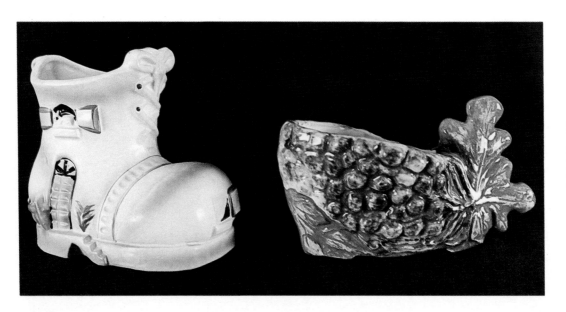

Left: Shoe house, 5" tall. Japan. $8.00 – 10.00. Right: Bunch of grapes, 7" long. Unmarked. $6.00 – 9.00.

Raggedy Ann and Andy

Raggedy Ann and Raggedy Andy are two of the best-loved characters in children's literature. 1995 marked Ann's 80th birthday. She was created by Johnny Gruelle, a political cartoonist and newspaper writer who was born in Arcola, Illinois. Johnny's daughter, Marcella, found her Grandmother's rag doll in their attic. In poor repair and with no facial features except for shoe-button eyes, Johnny drew a nose and smiling mouth on the doll and it became Marcella's favorite. Johnny began telling bedtime stories about Ann for his children. Tragically, at age 14, Marcella became ill and died. Her grieving father placed Ann on his desk and began writing down her adventures. Eventually, 38 books were published beginning in 1918 for Ann and in 1920, her sidekick, Andy, arrived. Johnny died in 1938 and his sons, Justin and Worth, continued publishing the stories. A grandson, Kim, keeps the Raggedys alive today.

Arcola is home base for an annual Raggedy Ann and Andy Festival held in May of each year. A Raggedy Ann collectors club flourishes and at least three books have been written on Raggedy collectibles. They are: "Enchanting Friends" by Dee Hockenberry, "Raggedy Ann and Raggedy Andy Family Album" by Susan Ann Garrison and "Raggedy Ann and Andy Collectibles" by Jan Lindenberger. Raggedy purists hunt for the original red-haired Anns and Andys, but many collectors also cherish most any rag doll piece.

Left: Raggedy Andy, 6⅜" tall. Marked Bobbs-Merrill 1976, Taiwan, Rubens. $12.00 – 15.00.
Right: Raggedy Ann, 6⅛" tall. Rubens is impressed on base. $12.00 – 15.00.

Two-sided Raggedy Andy, 5¾". This is his "I Am Happy Today" side. Rubens Original, Taiwan. $14.00 – 18.00.

This is the "I Am Sad Today" side of the two-sided Raggedy Andy. Same size and markings as at left. $14.00 – 18.00.

Left: Andy lying on his tummy, 4⅜" tall. Marked Rubens Original, Taiwan. $20.00 – 25.00. Right: Andy with baseball and bat, 6⅛". Marked Rubens, Japan. $20.00 – 25.00.

Left: Raggedy Ann, seated, 5¾". Rubens, Taiwan. $15.00 – 20.00. Right: Seated Raggedy Andy, 6¼". Rubens Originals, Taiwan. $15.00 – 20.00.

Left: Raggedys together, 6½" tall. Marked Bobbs-Merrill Co. Inc, 1976. Also Rubens Original, Japan. Bobbs-Merrill was the publisher of the Raggedy books. $15.00 – 20.00. Right: Blonde baby Raggedy, 5¼" tall. Marked NAPCOWARE Japan. $10.00 – 12.00.

Left: Blonde Raggedy Andy, 6⅛" tall. Marked RELPO, Japan. $12.00 – 15.00. Right: Raggedy Ann with star, 5" tall. Marked Bobbs-Merrill Co., (c) 1976, Japan. $12.00 – 15.00.

Blonde Raggedy Andy with bird, 6¼". Japan. $12.00 – 15.00.

Left: Mouse in wheat sheaf, 5¼" tall x 6¾" diameter. Right: 5¾" tall x 6". Both are marked Sylvac, Made in England and numbered 5245 and 5347, respectively. $30.00 – 35.00 each.

Squirrel with gold trim, 10" tall. Unmarked. $15.00 – 20.00.

Squirrel in nest, 4¾". This is a clay sculpture that weighs 2½ pounds! Unmarked. $7.00 – 9.00.

Left: Squirrel with pot, 3¾".
Unmarked. $6.00 – 8.00. Right:
Squirrel with cornucopia, 3⅝"
tall. Unmarked. $7.00 – 9.00.

Left: Squirrel on tree vase, gold trim, 8". Marked only
with the number 430 incised. $12.00 – 15.00. Right:
Teddy vase, 3¾". Stickers read Russ Harris & Co.
Taiwan #4403. $5.00 – 7.00.

Left: Squirrel in grass,
4½". Marked Ceramic
Fashions, O.P. Co., U.S.A.
$7.00 – 9.00. Right: Squir-
rel with acorn, 5¾".
Unmarked. $6.00 – 8.00.

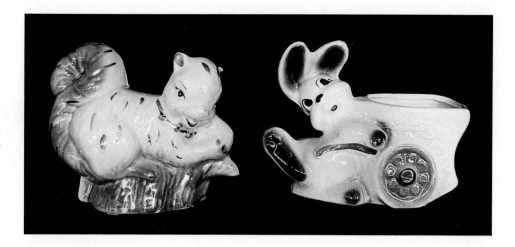

Left: Color variation of a squirrel in grass, this one with gold trim which raises the value of piece. $9.00 – 12.00. Right: Rabbit with cart, 5" tall. Unmarked. $8.00 – 10.00.

Bunny in garden, 5⅝". Sticker reads Royal, Japan, Hand Painted. $7.00 – 9.00.

Bunny house, 4½" tall. Lefton China. $15.00 – 18.00.

Left: Bunny in log, 8" long. American Bisque. $22.00 – 27.00. Right: Leaping bunny, 7¼" long. Unmarked. $12.00 – 15.00.

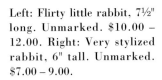

Left: Flirty little rabbit, 7½" long. Unmarked. $10.00 – 12.00. Right: Very stylized rabbit, 6" tall. Unmarked. $7.00 – 9.00.

Left: Leaping rabbit, 10" long. Marked 943, Made in USA. $10.00 – 12.00. Right: Seated rabbit, 8" long. Unreadable mark followed by #942. $8.00 – 10.00.

Left: Gardener rabbit, 9" long. American Bisque. $18.00 – 20.00. Right: Rabbit with removable carrot, 8" tall. Brush Pottery. $45.00 – 50.00.

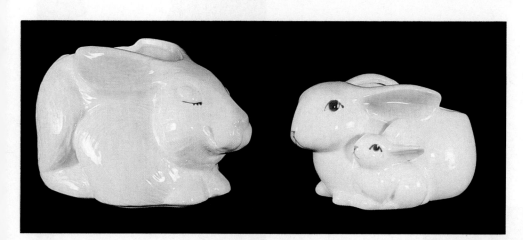

Left: Sleeping bunny, 9" long. McCoy Limited, USA. $15.00 – 18.00. Right: Mama rabbit with baby, 7" long. Unmarked. $9.00 – 12.00.

Left: Sleeping bunny with eggs, 10¼" long. Unmarked. $15.00 – 20.00. Right: Rabbit with carrot, 7½" tall. McCoy. $15.00 – 20.00.

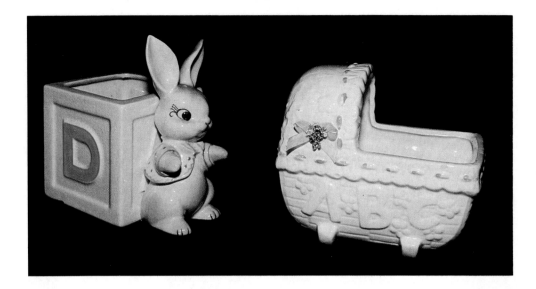

Left: Bunny with block, 6" tall. American Art Potteries. $8.00 – 10.00. Right: Bassinet, 6" long. Marked T-15200 Giftwares (c). $7.00 – 9.00.

Gentleman Easter bunny, 7¼" tall. Morton Pottery. $15.00 – 18.00.

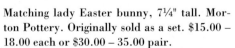

Matching lady Easter bunny, 7¼" tall. Morton Pottery. Originally sold as a set. $15.00 – 18.00 each or $30.00 – 35.00 pair.

Left: Bunny with tall basket, 4" tall. Unmarked. $8.00 – 9.00. Right: Variation of piece in top photo, page 79. Bunny with cart, 4½" tall. Unmarked. $8.00 – 10.00.

Left: Seated rabbit, 5½". Also comes in pink and aqua. Stanford Pottery. $12.00 – 14.00. Right: Bear at stump, 5½". American Bisque. $12.00 – 15.00.

Left: Tracking dog, 7¼" long. Unmarked. $7.00 – 9.00. Right: Reclining rabbit, 6" x 8". Marked Hollywood Floral Inc., Made in China. $8.00 – 10.00.

Left: Bunny with basket, 4½" tall. Unmarked. $5.00 – 7.00. Right: Elephant with raised trunk, 6" long. Unmarked. $5.00 – 7.00.

Demure little pink elephant with hairbow, 6" tall. Unmarked. $9.00 – 12.00.

Left: Jaunty walking elephant, 7¼" tall. Unmarked. $9.00 – 12.00. Right: Gold-trimmed elephant with basket, 5¼" tall. Unmarked. $12.00 – 15.00.

Elephant with lifted trunk, 7¾" tall. Beautiful glaze, but unmarked. $15.00 – 18.00.

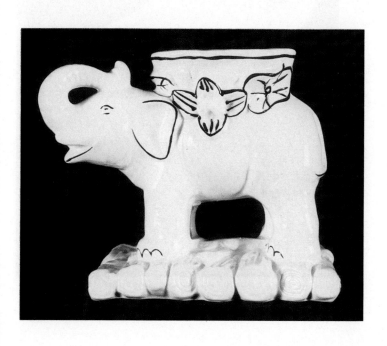

Elephant with howdah, 5¾" x 7¼". Black-stamped Hand Painted, Japan. $8.00 – 10.00.

Left: Little elephant with pot, 3¾" tall, gold trim. American Bisque. $12.00 – 14.00. Right: Resin elephant with tree stump, 4¼" tall. Unmarked. $7.00 – 9.00.

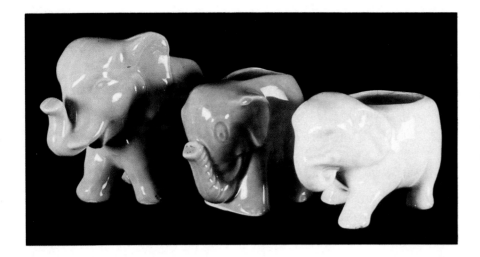

Three little elephants. Left: 5⅛" tall. Unmarked. $9.00 – 12.00. Center: 3¾" tall. Shawnee Pottery. $18.00 – 20.00. Right: 3½" tall. Unmarked. $7.00 – 9.00.

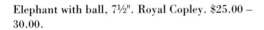

Elephant with ball, 7½". Royal Copley. $25.00 – 30.00.

Elephant with baby, 6" x 8". Beautiful detailing but unmarked. $18.00 – 22.00.

Bull elephant with base, 6" x 6½". Shawnee Pottery. $55.00 – 60.00 for this elusive fellow.

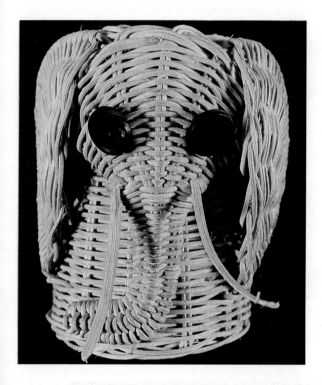

Wicker elephant, 5½" tall. What an odd-looking boy this is! $6.00 – 8.00. He has a glass container inside.

Dumbo planter, 6⅞" tall. This same mold has been made into a wall pocket by flattening the back somewhat and adding a hanging hole. Marked Dumbo, Walt Disney Productions and made by Leeds. $90.00 – 95.00. Leeds is a Chicago-based distributor licensed by Disney to use their characters in pottery pieces. Several potteries made the items for Disney, so pottery of origin is difficult to determine.

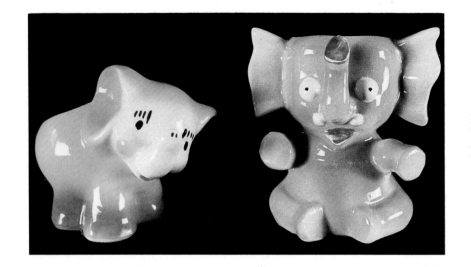

Left: Standing elephant, 5¼" long. Unmarked. $6.00 – 8.00. Right: Sitting elephant, 4½" tall. Unmarked. $6.00 – 8.00.

Left: Appealing little elephant with books, 5½" x 6½". Unmarked. $10.00 – 12.00. Right: Deer at stump, 5⅞" tall. Unmarked. $7.00 – 9.00.

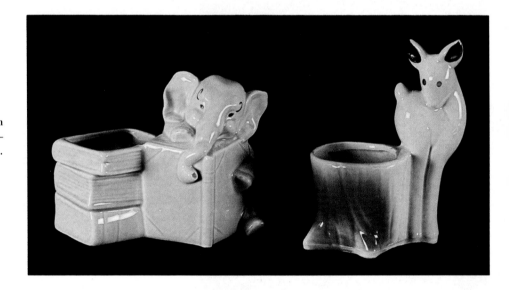

Left: Gold bear on log, 8" long. Unmarked. $10.00 – 12.00. Right: Reindeer with cart, 3½". Japan. $5.00 – 7.00.

Teddy bear in basket, 8" tall. Royal Copley. $45.00 – 50.00.

Polar bear with cub on ice floe, 10½" long. Great detailing on this piece, but unmarked. $18.00 – 22.00.

Left: Pudgy little bear at stump, 5¼" tall. Marked Made in California, B-1. $10.00 – 12.00. Right: Bears up a tree, 6⅝" tall. Unmarked. $8.00 – 10.00.

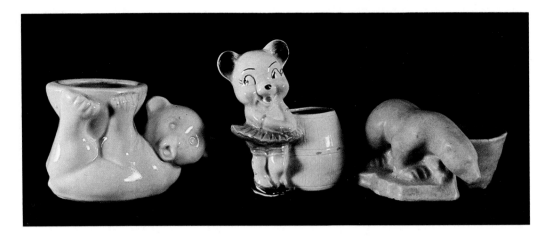

Left: Bear balancing a bowl on his feet, 6¼" long. Unmarked. $6.00 – 9.00. Center: Bear in tutu, 5¼" tall. Unmarked. $6.00 – 9.00. Right: Brown bear with pot, 5½" long. Niloak Pottery. $37.00 – 45.00.

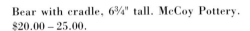

Bear with cradle, 6¾" tall. McCoy Pottery. $20.00 – 25.00.

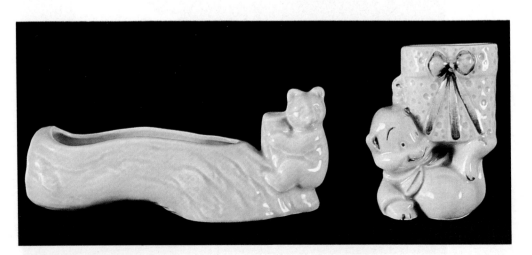

Left: Bear on log, 8½" long. Unmarked. $7.00 – 10.00. Right: Little bear balancing a package on his feet, 4½". Unmarked. $7.00 – 10.00.

Left: Woebegone bear, 5½".
Marked LCC USA which is the
mark used by McCoy after
being taken over by Lancaster
Colony Company. $12.00 –
15.00. Right: Bear with bees on
hive, 4¾" tall. Unmarked.
$9.00 – 12.00.

Left: Bear with hive, 5⅝" tall.
American Bisque. $18.00 –
20.00. Right: Bear with cart,
5¼" x 6". Unmarked. $9.00 –
12.00.

Left: Brown bear, 6¼" long.
Unmarked. $7.00 – 9.00. Right:
Twin bears, 6½" long. Haeger Pot-
tery. $12.00 – 15.00.

Left: Teddy bear with sucker, 8¼"
tall. Royal Copley. $35.00 – 38.00.
Right: Teddy bear with basket on
back. Royal Copley. $30.00 – 35.00.

Left: Bear in log, 7¼" long. American Bisque. $10.00 – 12.00. Right:
Bear with beehive. 5" tall, gold
trim. Unmarked. $12.00 – 14.00.

Left: Bear on log, 5½" tall. American Bisque. $12.00 – 14.00. Right:
Variation of bear with bees on hive,
4¾" tall. Unmarked except for the
number two. $10.00 – 12.00.

Left: Teddy bear on tree stump, 6¼"
tall. Royal Copley. $20.00 – 25.00.
Right: Teddy bear, 6½" tall. Royal
Copley. $25.00 – 28.00.

Left: Koala bear on stump, 5¼" tall.
Unmarked. $8.00 – 10.00. Right: Seal
with pot, 4½" tall. Niloak Pottery.
$30.00 – 35.00.

Left: Barking seal, 5¼" tall.
Unmarked. $10.00 – 12.00. Right:
Circus seal balancing a Christmas
ornament on his nose, 5¾" tall.
Unmarked. $10.00 – 12.00.

Left: Fox, 4¾" long. Unmarked. $7.00 – 9.00. Right: Stylized fox with big ears, 4¾". Unmarked. $7.00 – 10.00.

Fox on log with bunnies, 9" long. A beautiful bisque piece, nicely detailed and painted. Unmarked. $15.00. – 18.00.

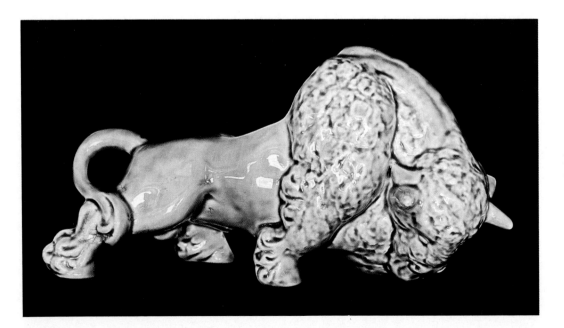

Bison, 10½" long. Marked only #269. $18.00 – 22.00.

Resting giraffe, 11½" tall. Marked Red
Wing Pottery with Joan Uhl signature.
$25.00 – 30.00.

Giraffe in leaves, 8¼" tall. Hull Pottery. Produced in the 1950s. $50.00 –
55.00.

Left: Monkey with nut, 5" tall.
Brush Pottery. $20.00 – 25.00.
Right: Monkey, 5½". NAPCO.
$9.00 – 12.00.

Left: Monkey with pot, 4½"
tall. Unmarked. $8.00 –
10.00. Right: Monkey scratch-
ing his head, 5". Brush Pottery. Marked USA 35A.
$18.00 – 22.00.

Left: Monkey head, 5½" tall.
McCoy Pottery. $12.00 –
15.00. Right: Monkey with
peanut, 4" tall. Unmarked.
$8.00 – 10.00.

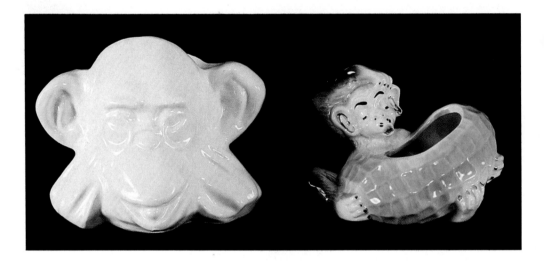

Left: Hound dog with finish of
tiny glass beads fused onto the
surface, 6¼" tall. Unmarked.
$8.00 – 10.00. Right: Monkey
with basket, 4½" tall. Japan.
$7.00 – 9.00.

Black whippet, 15" long. Unmarked but reminiscent of Stanford Ware. $15.00 – 18.00.

Left: Poodle with bow, 5½" tall. Unmarked. $8.00 – 10.00. Right: Poodle with cart, 8" long. Made in Japan. $8.00 – 10.00.

Left: Collie with basket, 4¾" tall. Unmarked. $8.00 – 10.00. Right: Very strange little fellow whith open mouth, 7½" long. RELPO Japan Hand Painted sticker. $7.00 – 9.00.

Dachshund, 15" long. Stanford Pottery in the late 1950s. $15.00 – 18.00.

Left: Dog with cart, 8¼" long. McCoy Pottery. $15.00 – 18.00. Right: Soulful dog, 7½" tall. Marked RELPO, Japan. $12.00 – 15.00.

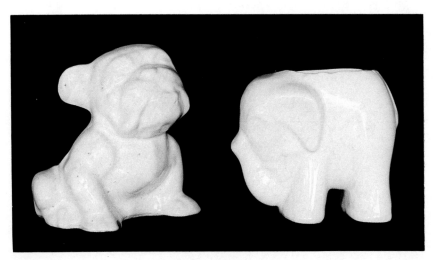

Left: Bulldog, 3½" tall. Morton Pottery. $6.00 – 8.00. Right: Elephant, 3". Brush McCoy. $10.00 – 12.00.

Left: Cocker with vase, 6¼" tall. Robinson-Ransbottom Co., #13020. $12.00 – 15.00. Right: Scottie dog planting dish, 8" long. McCoy Pottery. Introduced about 1949. $20.00 – 25.00.

Left: Bird dog planter/book-end, 5¾" x 6". McCoy USA. $25.00 – 30.00. From about 1955. Right: Dog dragging coat, 5¼" tall. McCoy Pottery. $18.00 – 20.00.

Dog with buggy, 8" long. Legend says "What About Me?" Decorated with 22 karat gold. McCoy Pottery. $20.00 – 22.00.

Dog in shoe, 7½" x 10". Haeger's sand finish. Bottom impressed Hound Dog Shoe Co (c) Haeger. There is even a hole in the sole of the shoe. $25.00 – 30.00.

Brown curly dog with basket, 8". Combination planter and TV lamp. Unmarked. $20.00 – 25.00.

Scottie dog, 11" long. Lovely coral color reminiscent of Brush but unmarked. $18.00 – 22.00.

Hunting dog, 12½" long. McCoy Pottery introduced about 1954. $55.00 – 60.00.

Dog and cat with spinning wheel, 7⅜". McCoy Pottery, introduced about 1953. $18.00 – 22.00.

Gingham dog, 4½". Marked Japan with wreath and blossom. $8.00 – 12.00.

Left: Dog with house, 4½".
Unmarked. $9.00 – 12.00.
Right: Dog on tray, 5¾" tall.
Unmarked. $9.00 – 12.00.

Left: Sad dog with basket, 4¼" tall.
Unmarked. $7.00 – 9.00. Right:
Earnest-looking puppy, 5" tall.
Unmarked. $8.00 – 10.00.

Left: Dog with shoe, 4¾".
Unmarked. $7.00 – 9.00. Right: Sit-
ting dog, 6¼" tall. Unmarked. $8.00
– 10.00.

Cocker lying down, 8¼" long. Shawnee Pottery. $12.00 – 15.00.

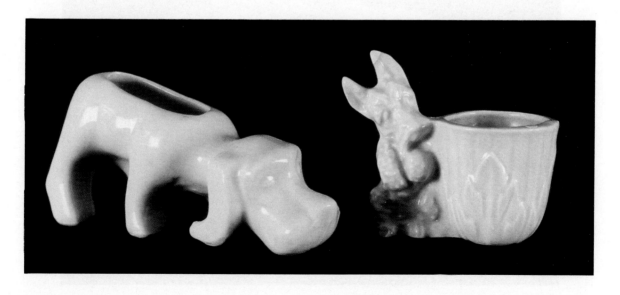

Left: Hound dog, 7" long. Shawnee Pottery. $8.00 – 10.00. Right: Scottie, 3¾". Unmarked. $6.00 – 8.00.

Left: Scottie with basket. Unmarked. $6.00 – 8.00. Center: Spaniel with basket, 5⅜". Royal Copley. $15.00 – 18.00. Right: Color variation of the Morton Pottery bulldog. $6.00 – 8.00.

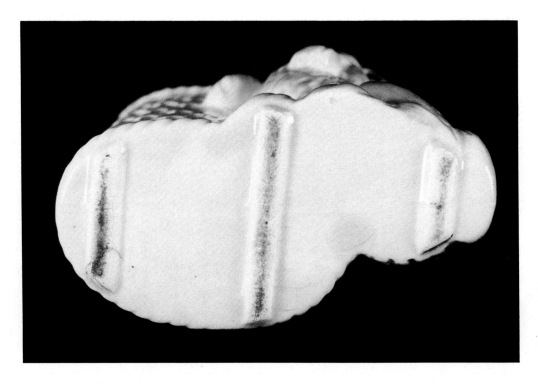

Base of the Royal Copley spaniel with basket shown above.

Left: Pup with ball of yarn, 6" x 7¾". Hull Pottery. $25.00 – 30.00. Right: Irish setter, 6½" tall. Shawnee Pottery. $10.00 – 12.00.

Left: Spaniel, 6¾" long. Brush McCoy. $18.00 – 20.00. Right: Demure little dog with flowers, 4¼" tall. Marked Block Pottery, California. $8.00 – 12.00.

Left: Scottie, 5½" tall Unmarked. $6.00 – 8.00. Right: Mutt, 5½". Unmarked. $6.00 – 8.00.

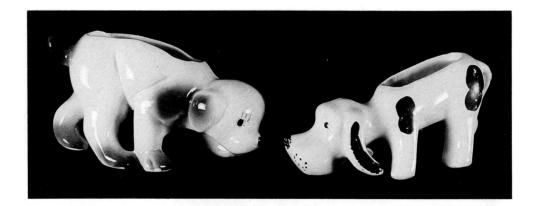

Left: Tracking dog, 7½" long. Variation in color of dog shown previously. Unmarked. $7.00 – 9.00. Right: Spotted hound dog, 7" long. Shawnee Pottery. $8.00 – 10.00.

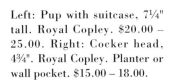

Left: Pup with suitcase, 7¼" tall. Royal Copley. $20.00 – 25.00. Right: Cocker head, 4¾". Royal Copley. Planter or wall pocket. $15.00 – 18.00.

White poodle planter. 7¼" tall. Royal Copley. $20.00 – 25.00.

Left: Dog pulling wagon, 6" x 7¼". Royal Copley. This is the one Leslie Wolfe named "Newbound" after us. $20.00 – 25.00. Right: Pup in basket, about 6¾" each way. $20.00 – 25.00.

Left: Dog at mailbox, 8" tall. Royal Copley. $15.00 – 18.00. Right: Seated cocker, 7½" tall. Royal Copley. $15.00 – 18.00.

Dog with cart, 6½" long. Made in Japan. $7.00 – 9.00.

Left: Lamb with bow, 6" x 9". Stanford Ware. $10.00 – 12.00. Right: Variation of dog with house, 5¾" tall. Unmarked. $8.00 – 10.00.

Left: Poodle with cart, 7" long. Unmarked. $7.00 – 9.00. Right: Donkey with cart, 7". Unmarked. $7.00 – 9.00.

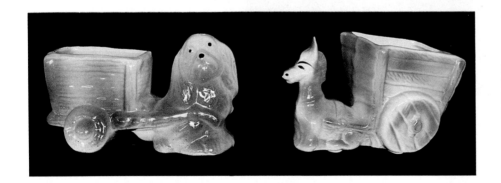

Left: Spaniel with cart, 3" x 6". Unmarked. $10.00 – 12.00. Right: Donkey with cart, 3½" x 6". Unmarked. $7.00 – 9.00.

Big-eyed puppy, 4¾" long. Unmarked. $7.00 – 9.00.

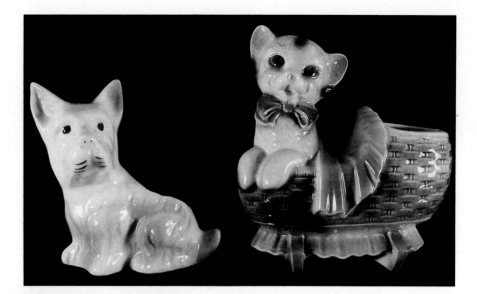

Left: Little pooch, 5¾". Unmarked. $6.00 – 8.00. Right: Kitten in cradle, 7½". Royal Copley. Fairly hard to find. $45.00 – 50.00.

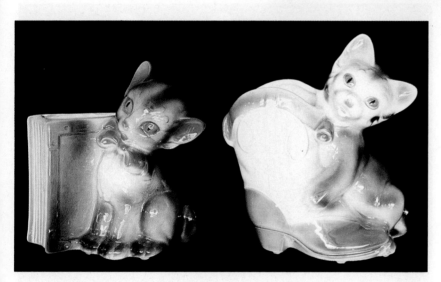

Left: Kitten and book, 6¼". Royal Copley. $20.00 – 25.00. Right: Kitten on boot. Royal Copley. $20.00 – 25.00.

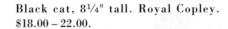

Black cat, 8¼" tall. Royal Copley. $18.00 – 22.00.

Left: Kitten with ball of yarn, 8". Royal Copley. $25.00 – 28.00. Right: Kitten in picnic basket. Royal Copley. $40.00 – 45.00.

Left: Cat with upraised paw, 6½" tall. The paw has a small hole in it, perhaps for an umbrella or something of that sort. Impressed Japan. $7.00 – 9.00. Right: This 7¼" tall cat with yarn is just like Royal Copley's, but the base is different. Marked USA 3026. Value not available.

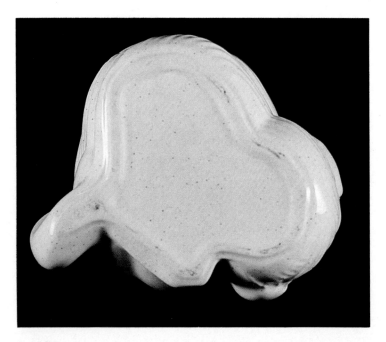

Base of the Copley-like white cat shown above.

Left: Cat with cello, 7⅞". Notice label on cello. An elusive piece. $60.00 – 65.00. Right: Black cat and tub, 5¼" tall. Royal Copley. $17.00 – 20.00.

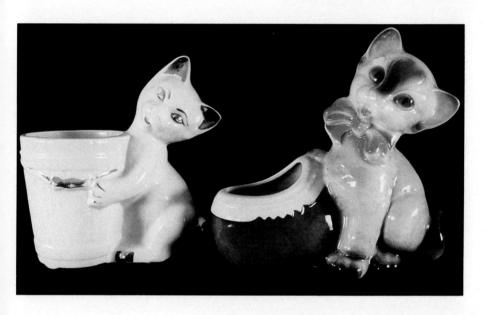

Left: White cat with bucket, 7", gold trim. Unmarked. $12.00 – 15.00. Right: Cat with moccasin, 8" tall. Royal Copley. $20.00 – 25.00.

Left: Cat with fish bowl, 5¾" x 7". American Bisque. $20.00 – 25.00. Right: Climbing cat, 6½" tall. Royal Copley. The base bars on this one are angled. $20.00 – 22.00.

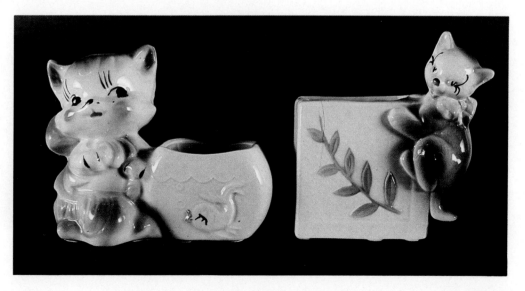

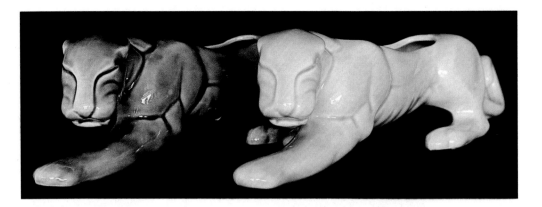

Green and yellow panthers, 16" long. Unmarked. $20.00 – 25.00.

King of the beasts, 9" x 12". Lovely big lion with ruby glass eyes. Marked L. E. Bowof(?) California (c). $18.00 – 22.00.

Black panther, 15" long. Possibly Stanford Ware. $12.00 – 15.00.

Left: Lion, 8½" long. McCoy, USA. $12.00 – 15.00. Right: Lioness, 10". McCoy. Combination planter and TV lamp. $20.00 – 25.00.

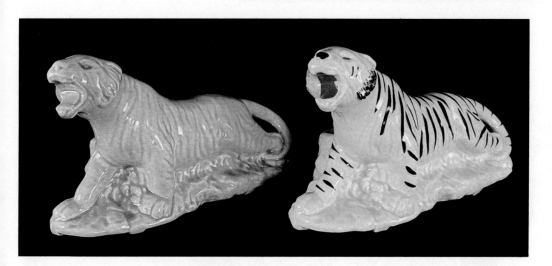

Pair of tigers, 10" long. One single color slip decorated, one hand painted. Unmarked. $10.00 – 14.00.

Base of tigers above.

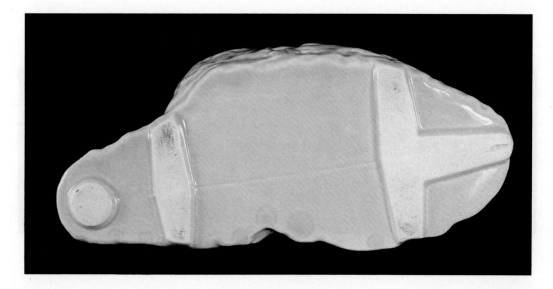

Lion, 14¼" long. McCoy. $18.00 – 22.00.

Left: Leaping tiger with leaves, 7¾" long. Brush type base. $15.00 – 20.00. Right: Lion with leaves, 5⅝" tall. Marked Stewart B. McCallum (c) California. $12.00 – 15.00.

Gold panther, 15" long. McCoy. The Sunburst Gold decoration was used from 1957 to about 1970 on various pieces. $22.00 – 25.00.

Left: Panther in leaves planter, 9½"
long. Panther figure is on both
sides. Unmarked. $12.00 – 15.00.
Right: Brown panther, 5¾" tall.
American Bisque. $20.00 – 25.00
plain, $25.00 – 30.00 with gold
trim.

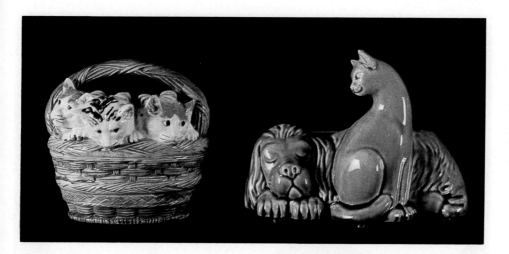

Left: Basketful of kittens, 5¼" x 5¾".
Black-stamped Japan. $15.00 –
20.00. Right: Cat and dog, 5¾" x 7½".
Unmarked but lovely detail and
design. $15.00 – 18.00.

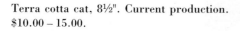

Terra cotta cat, 8½". Current production.
$10.00 – 15.00.

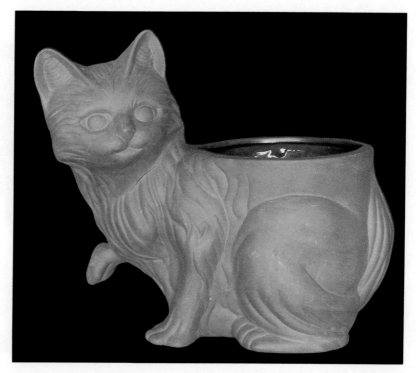

Left: Cat with basket, 5" long. Unmarked. $7.00 – 9.00. Right: Cat with back up, 2¾" tall. Midwest Pottery. $6.00 – 8.00.

Left: Seated cat, 5½". Brush Pottery. Mid 1950s. $35.00 – 40.00. Right: Cat with yarn, 6¾" long. Brush mark. $8.00 – 12.00.

Left: Loving cats vase, 6". Marked Brushcreek Creative Co. Applause, Inc. Made in China SKU54255. $9.00 – 12.00. Right: Yellow cat, 4½" long. Unmarked. $5.00 – 7.00.

Left: Seated cat with ribbon and bell, 5¾" tall. Marked T4808 inside bell. $8.00 – 10.00. Right: Black and white cat, 6½" long. Unmarked. $8.00 – 10.00.

Persian cat with bowl, 7½" tall. Hull Pottery. Introduced in the mid 1940s. $30.00 – 35.00.

Left: Persian cat, 4¼" tall. Looks very much like the Hull cat, but smaller and without the bowl. Unmarked. $8.00 – 10.00. Right: Stylized cat, 5¼" x 4". Unmarked. $6.00 – 9.00.

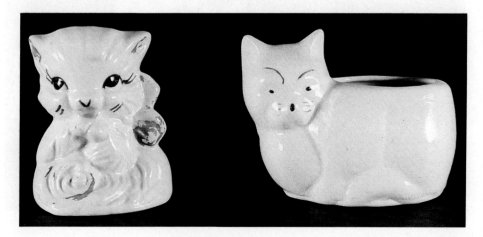

Left: Pair of Siamese cats, 6½" tall.
Unreadable markings. $10.00 – 12.00.
Right: Black and white cat, 6¼" tall.
Unmarked. $7.00 – 9.00.

Left: Reclining Siamese, 5½" x 7¾".
Unmarked. $8.00 – 10.00. Right:
Little Siamese, 5". Marked NAPCO-
WARE 6-6116. $6.00 – 9.00.

Left: Cat looking up, 3¼" tall.
Unmarked. $6.00 – 8.00. Right: Kitten
with basket and applied flowers, 4" x
5". Label Lefton #1923. $12.00 – 15.00.

Left: Cat with pot, 3¼" tall. USA. $5.00 – 7.00. Center: Cat, 2¾". May have had a lid. Sticker reads Nancy Lopez Inc., Made in Japan. $5.00 – 7.00. Right: Sitting cat, 4½" tall. Unmarked. $6.00 – 9.00.

Left: Seated cat, 4½" tall. Unmarked. $6.00 – 9.00. Center: Seated cat with painted accents, 3¾". Made in Canada. $6.00 – 8.00. Right: Calico cat, 4½" tall. Unreadable mark. $8.00 – 10.00.

Left: Gray kitty, 3⅛" tall. Red stamped Made in Japan. $5.00 – 7.00. Center: Cat with tail up, 4⅛". Unmarked. $5.00 – 7.00. Right: Cat with bowl on back, 2⅞" tall. Unmarked. $6.00 – 8.00.

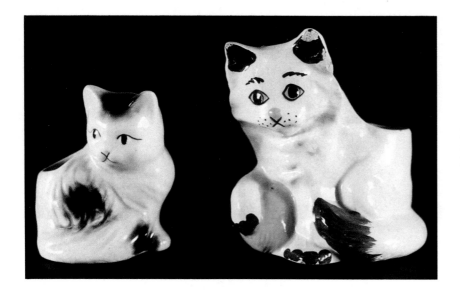

Left: Seated cat, 4¾". Unmarked. $6.00 – 8.00. Right: Cat with yarn ball, 6" tall. Unmarked. $7.00 – 9.00.

Left: Cat with polka-dot bow, 4¼" tall. Marked Grandcrest, Hand Painted, Japan. $10.00 – 12.00. Right: Cat, 4½" x 6¾". American Bisque. $12.00 – 14.00.

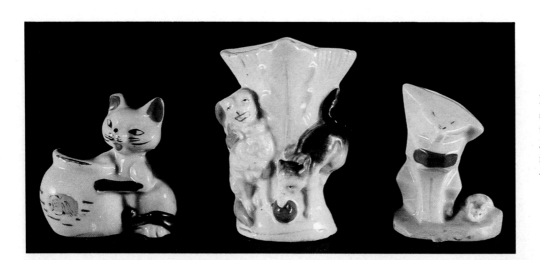

Left: Cat with pot, 2¾" tall. Black-stamped Japan. $5.00 – 7.00. Center: Cat and dog vase, 3¾" tall. Japan. $6.00 – 8.00. Right: Stylized cat, 3". Made in Japan. $5.00 – 7.00.

Kittens, one with gold and decal work and one blue with gold trim, 4½" tall. Unmarked. $8.00 – 10.00 each.

Left: Reclining cat with gingham checked bow, and glass eyes, 5" x 8". $8.00 – 10.00. Right: Seated cat with same gingham checked bow, 7" tall. Marked Taiwan. $8.00 – 10.00.

Left: Cat vase, 8¼" tall. Marked NAPCO on a palette shaped label. $7.00 – 9.00. Right: Cat with basket, 6¼" tall. McCoy Pottery from the mid 1940s. $12.00 – 15.00.

White cat hiding behind flower pot, 8" long. Unmarked. Cloth bow. $10.00 – 12.00.

Left: Baby rattle with kitten face, 6½" long. Marked NAPCOWARE Japan, C6700. $8.00 – 12.00. Right: Reclining happy cat, 6" long. Unmarked. $7.00 – 9.00.

Stack of three kittens, 3¾" tall. Unmarked. Came in a variety of colors and decorations. $9.00 – 12.00.

Left: Seated cat, 6¾" tall. Unmarked. $7.00 – 9.00. Right: Reclining cat, 4½" x 7½". Marked only USA, this is shown in both the McCoy and Shawnee books. $12.00 – 14.00.

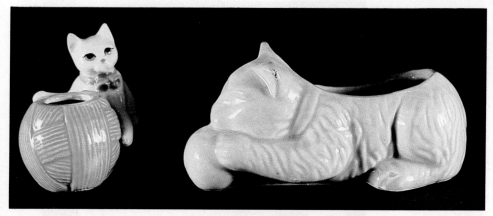

Left: Little kitten with big yarn ball, 2½" tall. Marked Schmid (c) 1979. $8.00 – 10.00. Right: Cat with ball, 5⅜" long. Unmarked. $7.00 – 9.00.

Left: Kitty with back up, 4½" long. Morton Pottery. $5.00 – 7.00. Center: Kitty, 5" long. Japan. $5.00 – 7.00. Right: Kitty, 4" long. Color variation of one on left. Morton Pottery. $5.00 – 7.00.

Pair of cats with basket, 6¾" x 10". Royal Haeger USA. Another example of their sand finish. $15.00 – 20.00.

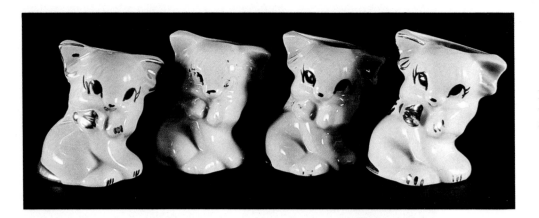

Four little kittens with various trims and colors, 4". Unmarked. $6.00 – 9.00 each.

Basket of kittens, 7½" tall. Unmarked. $10.00 – 12.00.

Left: Wailing kitten, 5½" tall. American Bisque. Will be found in various color combinations. $20.00 – 22.00. Right: Cat with shoe, 3¾" x 6". Brush Pottery. $20.00 – 25.00.

Left: Cat washing, 7" tall. Unmarked. $9.00 – 12.00. Right: Cat with yarn ball, 5¾" x 6". Pearl China Co., mid 1950s. $10.00 – 12.00.

Left: Cat in hat with spool, 6" x 7½". Unmarked. $10.00 – 12.00. Right: Cat with pot, 5" tall. Unmarked. $7.00 – 9.00.

Left: Siamese, 9" tall. Japan in wreath. $10.00 – 12.00. Right: Tiger kitten, 5" tall. Unmarked. $7.00 – 9.00.

Pair of Siamese in different colors, 6¼"
tall. Unmarked. $7.00 – 9.00 each.

Left: Gray kitten, 6⅜" tall. Unmarked.
$8.00 – 10.00. Right: Cat with washbas-
ket, 6¾" tall. McCoy Pottery. Comes in
several color variations from the mid
1940s. $12.00 – 15.00.

Left: Black cat with red, 6" tall. Shafford,
Japan. $10.00 – 12.00. Center: Cute black
kitten with much gold trim, 3⅞" tall.
Unmarked except for #17. $10.00 – 12.00.
Right: Black cat with open tummy, 5¼"
tall. Marked scouring pad holder, Taiwan.
$7.00 – 9.00.

Left: Fat cat, 2¼". Lefton. $7.00 – 9.00. Next: 2⅞" tall. Japan. $6.00 – 8.00. Right: 3⅞" tall. Made in Occupied Japan with horseshoe mark. $12.00 – 14.00.

Left: Kitty with hat, 6¼" tall. Hull Pottery, 1950s. $30.00 – 35.00. Right: Kitty with leaves, 3¼" tall. Japan. $7.00 – 9.00.

Left: Stylized black and white cat, 3" tall. Black-stamped Made in Japan. $7.00 – 9.00. Right: Tan lustre cat with pot, 3¼" tall. Japan. $10.00 – 12.00.

Left: Sleeping cat, 2½" x 6¼". American Bisque. $8.00 – 10.00. Right: Cat and mouse with bucket, 2½" tall. Unmarked. $7.00 – 9.00.

Left: Cat at well, 5½". Resin material, fairly current. Unmarked. $7.00 – 9.00. Right: Cat on divan, 6¾" long. Unmarked. Great detail! $9.00 – 12.00.

Left: Blue and white cat, 4¾". Marked Grantcrest, Hand Painted, Japan. $6.00 – 8.00. Right: Cat in watering can, 5¼" tall. Made in Japan. $7.00 – 9.00.

Left: Cat with basket, 4¾".
Black-stamped Hand Painted,
Japan. $7.00 – 9.00. Right:
Playful cat, 4" x 6". Gold trim.
Marked Shafer 23K Gold Guar-
anteed. $10.00 – 12.00.

Left: Stack of kittens, 4½" x 7".
Resin material, fairly new.
Unmarked. $8.00 – 10.00.
Right: Cat with pink ears, 4⅝"
tall. Unmarked. $8.00 – 10.00.

Cat on tricycle with planter pot,
7⅜" tall. Unmarked. $12.00 –
15.00.

Left: Black cat with glass goldfish bowl, 6¾". Camark Pottery. $30.00 – 35.00. Right: Siamese with glass fish bowl, 7¼" tall. Marked Marston, California. $20.00 – 25.00.

Black cats with pots. Left: 2⅜" tall. Right: 2¾" tall. Redware. Attributed to Occupied Japan. $12.00 – 15.00 each.

Left: Mama cat with baby, 6½". Japan. $8.00 – 10.00. Right: Gray and white cat, 3¾" x 6¼". Unmarked. $7.00 – 9.00.

Cat with spinning wheel, 6¾" x 7¼" long. McCoy USA. Notice the cat is sitting on a locked suitcase with the initials R.S. on it. Mysterious! Introduced about 1953. This will also be found with a white dog sitting up and looking at the cat. This particular piece never had the dog, although the hole is there (lower left) for his chain. $15.00 – 20.00.

Kitty at well, 8½" long. McCoy Pottery from mid 1950s. Legend says "Stung by the Splendor of a Sudden Thought." $20.00 – 25.00.

Left: Cat and fiddle, 6½". Unmarked. $8.00 – 10.00. Right: Smiley cat, 7". Unmarked. $6.00 – 9.00.

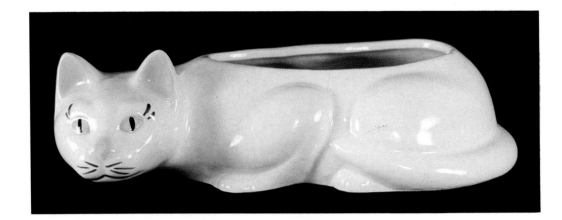

White cat, 10¾" long. Unmarked. $10.00 – 12.00.

Left: Seated cat, 8". Brush Pottery. $45.00 – 50.00. Right: Persian cat, 7" tall. Unmarked. $8.00 – 10.00.

Left: Cats with wash basket, 7¼" tall. This is another variation in color and trim of this charming piece by McCoy Pottery. Gold trim raises value. $20.00 – 25.00. Right: Cat and dog at stump, 4¾". American Bisque. $16.00 – 18.00.

Left: Gray cat head, 5" tall. McCoy. Marked #617 LCC, USA. $12.00 – 15.00. Right: Cat with ball of yarn, 7½". This is another of those Royal Copley look-alikes only this time by McCoy. See first two photos page 110. Marked McCoy, USA, LCC, 3026. $12.00 – 15.00.

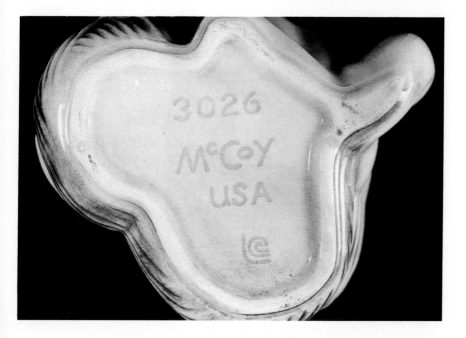

Base of the cat with ball of yarn above.

Left: Cat with basket, 6⅛" tall. McCoy Pottery. Marked NM in small letters. Color variation of piece shown before. $12.00 – 15.00. Right: Reclining Persian cat, 10" long. Morton Pottery. $15.00 – 18.00.

Left: Mama cat with kitten, 9" tall. Marked only USA. $10.00 – 12.00. Right: Kangaroo, 7". Unmarked. $7.00 – 9.00.

Cloth-covered cat, 11" tall. This has pottery base, covered with fabric and varnished. Marked Royal Trimmings by Clewls, Cookson Pottery, Roseville. $10.00 – 12.00.

Left: Camel, 5½". Brush Pottery. $18.00 – 20.00. Right: Kangaroo with baby in pouch, 6¾". Unmarked. $7.00 – 9.00.

Left: Kangaroo, 5¾". Unmarked. $7.00 – 9.00. Right: Elephant with trunk lifted, 5¼". Unmarked. $6.00 – 8.00.

Left: Doe and fawn heads on base, 6" x 7¾". Unmarked. $10.00 – 12.00. Right: Kangaroo with baby, 6½". Color variation. Unmarked. $8.00 – 10.00.

Stylized white deer, 7½" long. Unmarked. $7.00 – 9.00.

Fawn and log, 6¾" tall. Shawnee Pottery. $35.00 – 40.00.

Deer with leaves, 11½" long. Much gold and beautiful detail but unmarked. $30.00 – 35.00.

Fawn vase, 9⅜" tall. McCoy Pottery. $20.00 – 25.00.

Deer with fawns, 12" long. McCoy, mid 1950s. $35.00 – 40.00.

Left: Box with deer figure, 7¼" tall. Unmarked. $9.00 – 12.00. Right: Deer vase, 8¾". Dryden Pottery in Arkansas. $15.00 – 20.00.

Running deer TV lamp and planter, 10½". Unmarked. $15.00 – 20.00.

Unicorn vase, 10" tall. Impressed script, Hull USA. 98. $55.00 – 65.00.

Left: Deer with flower collar, 5". Unmarked. $7.00 – 9.00. Right: Leaping goat, 6½" tall. Unmarked. $10.00 – 12.00.

Running deer planter and TV lamp, 4½" x 10½". Color variation of piece shown on page 137. Unmarked. $15.00 – 20.00.

Left: Reclining deer, 4½" tall. McCoy Pottery about 1940. $18.00 – 20.00. Right: Deer and fawn, 6". Shawnee Pottery. Marked #669. $20.00 – 25.00.

Bambi with bowl, 5¾" x 10". Leeds, probably produced by American Bisque. Leeds was a jobber licensed to make Disney character pieces in pottery. Different potteries produced them so it is difficult to assign ownership. $25.00 – 30.00.

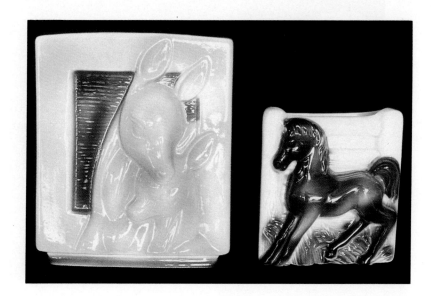

Left: Deer and doe planter, 6½" x 7½". Royal Copley. $12.00 – 15.00. Right: Pony at fence, 5½" tall. Royal Copley. $10.00 – 12.00.

Left: Deer and fawn, 5½" x 6¼". Royal Copley. $15.00 – 18.00. Right: Deer open vase, 7½" x 7". Royal Copley. $15.00 – 18.00.

Left: Doe and fawn with side planter, 7" x 8". Royal Copley. $20.00 – 25.00. Right: Full-bodied deer on stump. Royal Copley. $20.00 – 25.00.

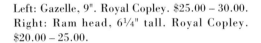

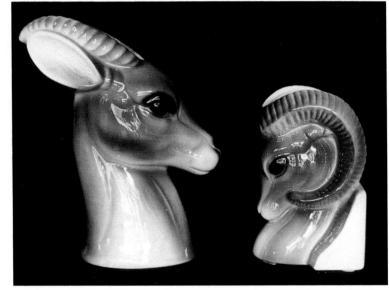

Left: Gazelle, 9". Royal Copley. $25.00 – 30.00. Right: Ram head, 6¼" tall. Royal Copley. $20.00 – 25.00.

Left: Deer and fawn, 9¼". Royal Copley. $20.00 – 25.00. Right: Little deer head vase, 7" tall. Royal Copley. This one is hard to find. $25.00 – 30.00.

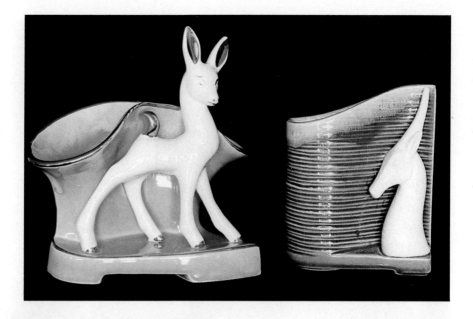

Left: White deer on vase, 8" tall. Marked Shafer 23K Gold Guaranteed. $18.00 – 22.00. Right: Impala on vase, 6¼". Unmarked. $8.00 – 10.00.

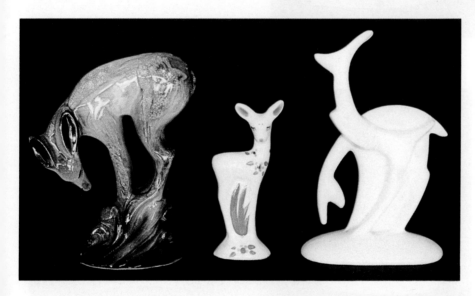

Left: Standing Deer, 6½". Unmarked but lovely! $20.00 – 25.00. Center: Deer with painted trim, 4¾" tall. Unmarked. $6.00 – 9.00. Right: Pair stylized deer, 6¾" tall. Haeger Pottery. $20.00 – 25.00.

Left: Bambi with leaves, 4½" tall. By Leeds for Disney. $15.00 – 20.00. Right: Deer on pull toy. 7" tall. Japan. $8.00 – 10.00.

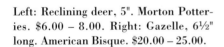

Left: Leaping deer, 10". Unmarked. $10.00 – 12.00. Right: Buck standing, 11". Marked Maddux of California, 526. $20.00 – 25.00.

Left: Reclining deer, 5". Morton Potteries. $6.00 – 8.00. Right: Gazelle, 6½" long. American Bisque. $20.00 – 25.00.

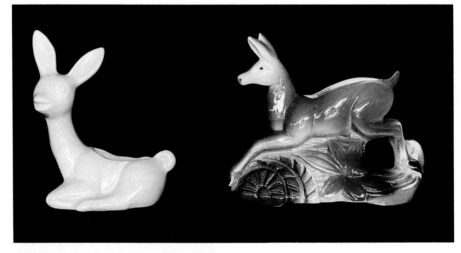

Left: Brown and white reclining deer. Right: Same deer, white. Marked Originals in Stanford Ware, Sebring, Ohio. $12.00 – 14.00 each.

Left: Running deer, 6". Unmarked. $10.00 – 12.00. Right: Deer, 7". Shawnee Pottery. $8.00 – 10.00.

Left: Fawn and stump, 7⅛" tall. Shawnee Pottery. $16.00 – 18.00. Right: Monkey with peanut, 4" x 5¼". Unmarked. $8.00 – 10.00.

Left: Deer at wall, 5½". Unmarked. $7.00 – 9.00. Right: Prancing goat, 5¼" tall. Unmarked. $7.00 – 9.00.

Donkey and elephant at well, 8¼" long. Samson Import Co., 1969. #5455. $40.00 – 45.00.

Left: Reclining horse, 6½" long. Shown both American Bisque and Shawnee books. Unmarked. $10.00 – 12.00. Right: Donkey with saddle baskets and owner at siesta, 6" tall. Unmarked. $8.00 – 10.00.

Left: Bashful donkey, 5¾" tall. American Bisque marked USA. $10.00 – 12.00. Right: Donkey with cart, 4¾". Marked USA. Probably American Bisque. $10.00 – 12.00.

Toy zebra, 8" tall. Marked only S677/2. $10.00 – 12.00.

Left: Mare and colt, 5½" tall. Unmarked. $8.00 – 10.00. Right: Rearing dark horse with much gold trim, 6⅛" tall. Marked Ceramic Fashions, O.P. Co. USA. $10.00 – 12.00.

Left: Horse with circus wagon, 9" long. Unmarked. $10.00 – 12.00. Right: Donkey with basket, 5¼". Shawnee Pottery. Marked USA. $25.00 – 30.00.

Left: Sway-backed horse with hat, 6".
Brush Pottery. $20.00 – 25.00. Right:
Cow with calf, 4" tall. Brush Pottery.
$20.00 – 25.00. This coral color is
Brush's own.

White mare with foal, 11½" long.
Brush Pottery. $35.00 – 40.00.

Mare and colt, 9" long. Unmarked but
great detail and coloring. $20.00 –
25.00.

Burro with basket, 10" tall. Unmarked. $12.00 – 18.00.

Rocking horse, 8" long. Legend on one side says "Ride a Cock Horse" on the other side, "To Banbury Cross." McCoy Pottery. $20.00 – 25.00. Introduced in 1955.

Mare zebra with colt, 9". McCoy Pottery. $40.00 – 50.00. Introduced in 1956.

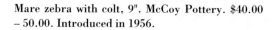

Left: Circus horse, 7" tall. Unmarked. $10.00 – 12.00. Right: Toy horse, 7¼". Pearl China. $10.00 – 12.00.

Left: Dromedary, 5" tall. Marked only USA 963. $10.00 – 12.00. Right: Reclining Bactrian camel, 3¼" x 5½". Niloak. $40.00 – 45.00.

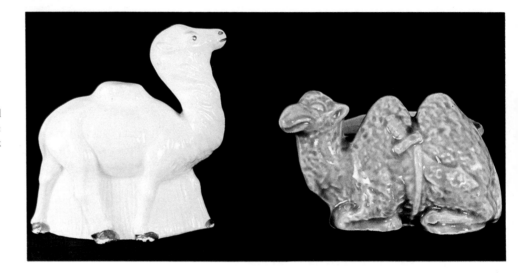

Left: Reclining zebra, 5¼" tall. Unmarked. $10.00 – 12.00. Right: Standing zebra, 5½". Unmarked. $10.00 – 12.00.

Left: Rearing circus horse, 6¾"
tall. American Bisque. $30.00 –
35.00. Right: Toy horse, 7".
Shawnee. $18.00 – 20.00.

Left: Rearing horse, 9" tall. Unmarked.
$15.00 – 20.00. Right: Ram head vase,
9½" tall. McCoy Pottery. $45.00 – 50.00.
Introduced in late 1940s – early 1950s.

Left: Rearing horse, 9½" tall. Planter
in back. Unmarked but lovely detail
and glaze. $20.00 – 25.00.

Base of horse planter shown in bottom photo, page 149.

Left: Stylized horse, 3¾" x 5". Marked only USA. $7.00 – 9.00. Right: Standing horse, 6" tall. Morton Pottery. $10.00 – 12.00.

Left: Stylized little horse, 5½". McCoy Pottery. $15.00 – 20.00. Right: Rearing horse, 6". Shawnee Pottery. $18.00 – 20.00.

Left: Donkey with cart, 5¼" long. Japan. $6.00 – 8.00. Right: Donkey with keg, 4½" x 6". Japan. $7.00 – 9.00.

Big black bull, 10½" long. Very stylized. Unmarked. History shows us that the time when sculpture and art became stylized marked the end of many civilizations. Cheerful thought, isn't it? $12.00 – 15.00.

Left: Calf, 4½" tall. Morton Potteries. $10.00 – 12.00. Right: Cow standing on her teat, 4¼". Ouch! Japan. $7.00 – 9.00.

Left: Donkey with cart, 8" long. Shawnee Pottery. $9.00 – 12.00. Right: Calf, 6½" long. McCoy Pottery about 1943. $10.00 – 12.00.

Stagecoach garden dish, 12" long. Brush Pottery. $35.00 – 40.00.

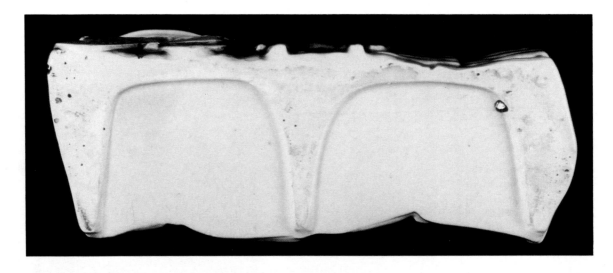

Base of above Brush Pottery piece.

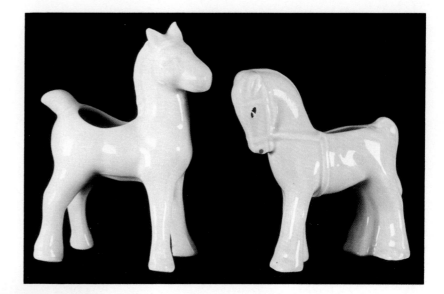

Left: Horse, 6¼" tall. Morton Pottery.
$7.00 – 9.00. Right: Standing horse, 5¼"
tall. Shawnee Pottery. $12.00 – 15.00.

Left: Pair of flirty looking donkeys, 6" tall.
Unmarked. $9.00 – 12.00. Right: Horse,
3⅜" tall. Unmarked. $6.00 – 9.00.

Horse with mane vase, 8" tall. Royal Copley. Also in brown with black mane which
is harder to find. $20.00 – 25.00.

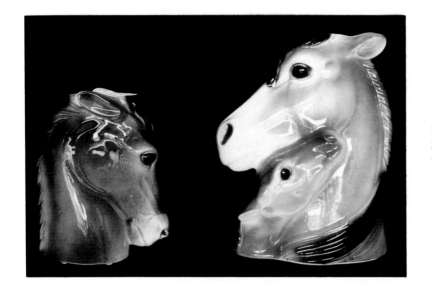

Left: Horse head, 6" tall. Royal Copley. $16.00 – 18.00. Right: Horse and colt, 8¼" tall. Royal Copley. $25.00 – 30.00.

Left: Running horse, 7¼" x 7". Marked Joan Lea. $10.00 – 15.00. Right: Rocking horse, 6¼" x 7½". Stanford Ware. $10.00 – 12.00.

Left: Donkey with cart, 6" tall. Unmarked. $8.00 – 10.00. Right: Whimsical donkey with cart, 6¾" tall. American Bisque. Looks a lot like its partner, but a little different in size. $12.00 – 14.00.

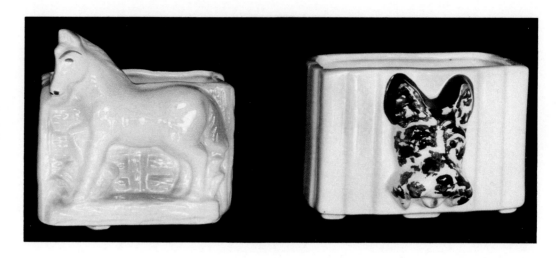

Left: Horse at wall, 4" tall. Unmarked. $6.00 – 9.00. Right: Scottie head, 3½" x 5". Unmarked. $7.00 – 9.00.

Left: Donkey with cart, 6¾" x 8". Marked INARCO, Japan, E3616. $6.00 – 8.00. Right: Lamb, 5¾" tall. Marked © Samson Import Co. 1961, 4315 Japan. $6.00 – 8.00.

Left: Raccoon on log, 6½". Brush Pottery. $35.00 – 40.00. Right: Horse at tree stump, 3½" tall. Unmarked. $10.00 – 12.00.

Left: Puppies on log, 6¼" long. Brush. $35.00 – 45.00. Right: Cat and dog on log, 6" long. Marked Shafer 24K Gold. Brush. $45.00 – 50.00.

Left: Bunny on log, 6" long. Brush Pottery. $35.00 – 40.00. Right: Squirrels on log, 6½" long. Brush. $35.00 – 45.00.

Left: Hen on log with rooster, 6½" long. Brush Pottery. $35.00 – 45.00. Right: Bear on log, 6½" long. Brush Pottery. $35.00 – 45.00.

Left: Black bear in log, 6½". Unmarked. $20.00 – 22.00. Right: Skunk on log, 5½" long. Unmarked. $15.00 – 18.00.

Left: Very round little pig, 4¼" long. Shawnee, USA #760. $12.00 – 14.00. Right: Pig moving barrel, 5¼" tall. Unmarked. $10.00 – 12.00.

Left: Little pig with box, 5⅝" tall. Unmarked. $7.00 – 9.00. Right: Clown riding pig, 8½" long. McCoy Pottery, introduced about 1951. $18.00 – 20.00.

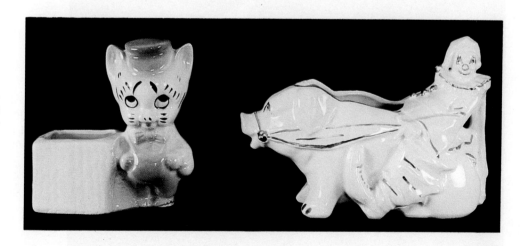

Left: Pig with apple, 5¼" tall. Unmarked. $7.00 – 9.00. Right: Farmer pig with corn, 6⅛" tall. American Bisque. $8.00 – 10.00.

Left: Three pigs at wall, 4⅛" x 5½". Shawnee, USA. $12.00 – 14.00. A planter almost exactly like this was made by Morton Pottery except that all the pigs' heads are above the wall. Right: Flower decorated pig, 5" long. Unmarked. $6.00 – 9.00.

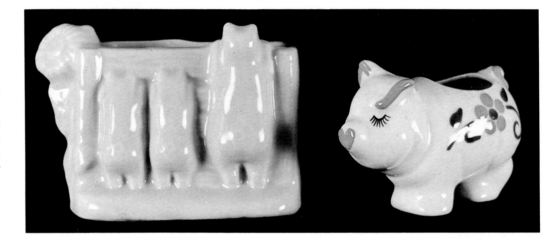

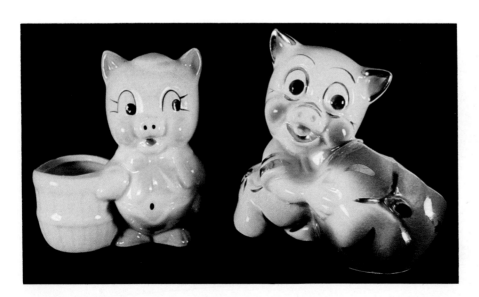

Left: Pig with basket, 4¾". Unmarked. $8.00 – 10.00. Right: Pig with apple, gold trim, 5½". Unmarked. $10.00 – 12.00.

Left: Pig with clover, 6". American Bisque. $8.00 – 10.00. Right: Pig with book, 5" x 7". Title of book is "Three Little Pigs." American Bisque. $22.00 – 25.00.

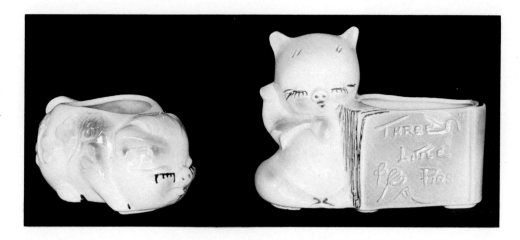

Left: Pig with cart, 5½", Gold trim. Unmarked. $8.00 – 10.00. Right: Pig with gold trimmed cart. Unmarked. $8.00 – 10.00.

Left: Reclining lamb, 3¾" tall. Unmarked. $7.00 – 9.00. Right: Pig at well, 5¼". Much decoration. Unmarked. $8.00 – 10.00.

Cutie pie lamb, 11". American Bisque. $30.00 – 35.00.

Left: Curly sheep, 6". McCoy Pottery. Marked NM. $12.00 – 15.00. Right: Sheep with lamb, 4¾" tall. Legend says "Ba Ba Black Sheep." McCoy Pottery. $12.00 – 15.00.

Left: Lamb with bow, 7¼" tall. McCoy USA. Early 1950s. $15.00 – 18.00. Right: Lambs jumping fence, 7" tall. Haeger USA. $12.00 – 15.00.

Left: Demure lamb, 7¼" tall. Unmarked. $7.00 – 9.00. Right: Frolicking lamb, 6¾" tall. Royal Haeger. $10.00 – 12.00.

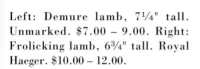

Left: Sleeping lamb, 5¾" long. Unmarked. $7.00 – 9.00. Right: Lamb with bells, 7¼" tall. McCoy Pottery, late 1940s. $12.00 – 15.00.

Big lamb, 10¾" long. American Bisque. $35.00 – 40.00. Also made in 12½" size.

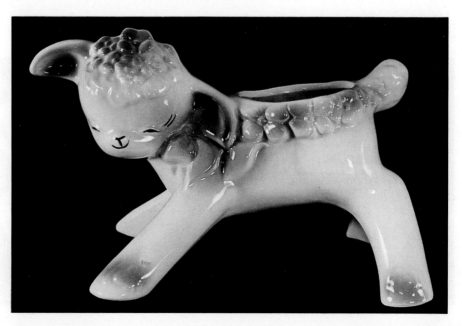

Lamb with bow, 6¾" x 9¼". Unmarked.
$12.00 – 15.00.

Left: Reclining sheep with gold trim,
4" x 6". Unmarked. $10.00 – 12.00.
Right: Black sheep, 4⅝" x 6¼".
Unmarked. $8.00 – 10.00.

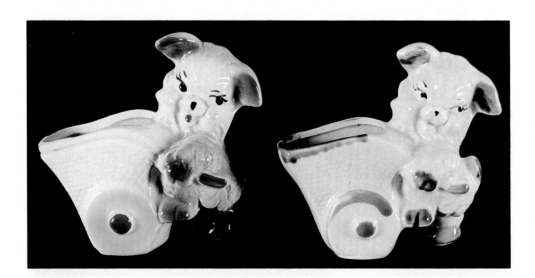

Two color variations of the same
lamb with garden cart, 5½" tall.
Unmarked. $9.00 – 12.00 each.

Left: Lamb with pink bow, 7½" x 10". Stanford Ware. $12.00 – 14.00. Right: Lamb on rocker, 6" x 7½". Stanford Ware. $12.00 – 14.00.

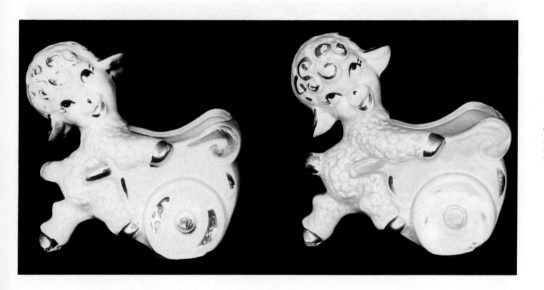

Two color variations of lamb with buggy, 5¾" tall, gold trim. Unmarked. $8.00 – 10.00 each.

Left: Reclining sheep, 7" long. Unmarked. $7.00 – 9.00. Right: Reclining cow, 5½" long. Japan. $5.00 – 7.00.

Left: Standing lamb, 6". Unmarked. $6.00 – 9.00. Right: Rooster with bucket, 6¼" long. Unmarked. $7.00 – 9.00.

Left: Smiling lamb, 6". Stanford. $10.00 – 12.00. Right: Cocker, 5¼". Unmarked. He must have been chasing the lamb in order to get in this section! $6.00 – 8.00.

Left: Bunny with cabbage, 6". Unmarked. $7.00 – 9.00. Right: Lamb with flower, 6". McCoy Pottery, mid 1940s. $10.00 – 12.00.

Left: Ram, 4¾" x 6". Sticker says Tahaha Shi, San Francisco, Made in Japan. $7.00 – 9.00. Right: Snail at stump, 3¼" x 5¾". Unmarked. $6.00 – 8.00.

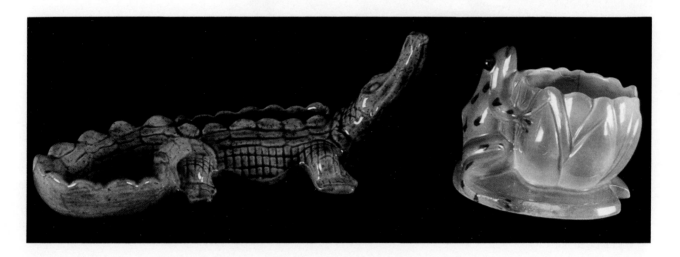

Left: Alligator planter, 9¾". Very cute piece marked "To Grandpa From Linda," evidently a ceramic class item. $7.00 – 9.00. Right: Frog with lotus, 3¾". Marked USA. $7.00 – 9.00.

Bowl, 15¾". Hull Pottery, Ebb Tide Line, 1954. This is a gorgeous piece and can be found in various colors. $90.00 – 100.00.

Left: Frog singing "Valencia," 7" tall. Marked Germany. $12.00 – 15.00. Center: Frog with tennis shoes, 5¼" long. Unmarked. $7.00 – 9.00. Right: Turtle with tennis shoes, 5½". Unmarked. $7.00 – 9.00.

Caterpillar, 14". Marked Floraline, USA. Also LCC #0416, McCoy Pottery after Lancaster Colony took over. $15.00 – 20.00.

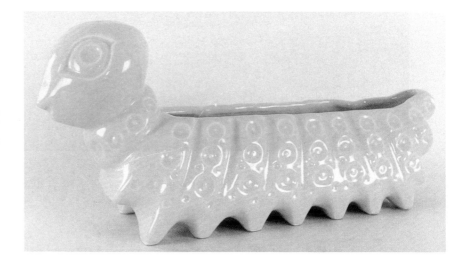

Monster snail, 7½" x 11½". LCC (Lancaster Colony) #545 by McCoy Pottery. $15.00 – 20.00.

Left: Snail, 7" long. Marked R.R.P. Co., #415 (Robinson-Ransbottom of Roseville, Ohio). $15.00 – 20.00. Right: Bug, 7" long. Marked #419 R.R.P. Co. $15.00 – 20.00.

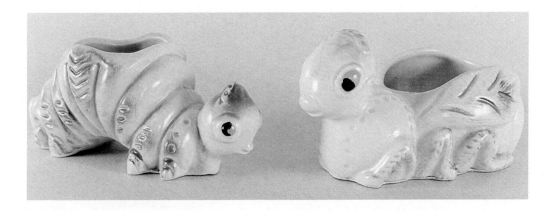

Left: Inchworm, 6¾" long. Marked R. R. P. Co., Roseville, Ohio, #418. $15.00 – 20.00. Right: Beetle bug, 6¾" long. Marked R.R.P. Co., Roseville, Ohio. #417. $15.00 – 20.00.

Sailfish with net, 8½" x 10½". American Bisque. $45.00 – 50.00.

Sailfish on waves, 8" x 11". American Bisque.
$45.00 – 50.00.

Left: Fantail fish, 5¾" long. Marked
PIERNO Original. $6.00 – 9.00.
Right: Mermaid with shell, 7¼" long.
Brush Pottery. Marked. #245. $25.00
– 30.00.

Seahorse in waves, 10¾" long. Brush
Pottery. $35.00 – 40.00.

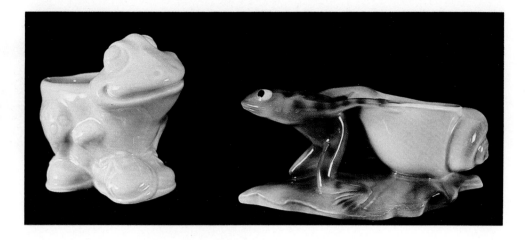

Left: Frog, 5¾". Unmarked. $6.00 – 9.00. Right: Frog with shell, 7¼" long. Marked Clay Sketches, Pasadena, So. Ca. $9.00 – 12.00.

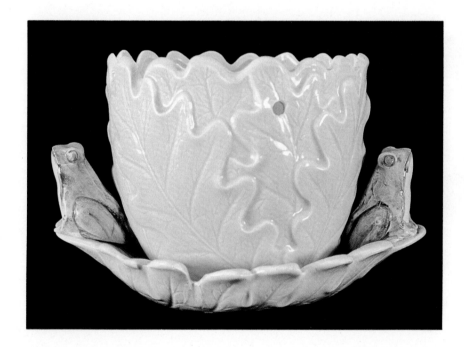

Frogs with oak leaf bowl, 5" x 7¾". Unmarked. $12.00 – 15.00.

Left: Turtle with leaves. McCoy Pottery, about 1950. $12.00 – 15.00. Right: Standing turtle, 6⅛" tall. Unmarked. $9.00 – 12.00.

Pair of alligators, both McCoy Pottery. Left is 9½" long; Right is 10" long. $18.00 – 22.00 each.

Left: Fighting frog, 10" long. He's missing some teeth, but has one gold one and a patch over one eye. Unmarked. $18.00 – 22.00. Right: Frog on shell, 4¾" tall. Niloak Pottery. $40.00 – 45.00.

Left: Frog, 8¼" long. Brush Pottery. $20.00 – 30.00. Right: Frog with chin on hand, 10" long. Brush Pottery. $50.00 – 55.00.

Left: Frog with banjo, 5¼" tall. Unmarked. $9.00 – 12.00. Right: Frog musicians, 5" long. Brush Pottery. Marked #512 USA. $15.00 – 20.00.

Frog with umbrella, 7½" long. McCoy Pottery. The umbrella is a loose piece on a wire stem. Introduced about 1954. $45.00 – 50.00.

Left: Frog in leaves, 5½". McCoy Pottery, about 1949. $12.00 – 15.00. Right: Frog, 6¼" long. Brush Pottery. $25.00 – 35.00.

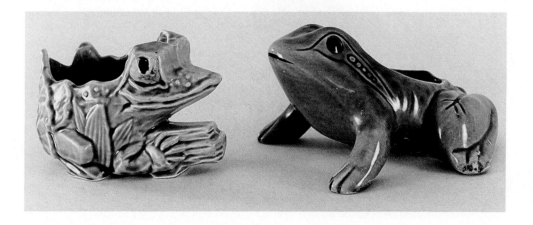

Left: Toad with leaves, 7½". McCoy. $12.00 – 15.00. Right: Frog with flowers, 7½". McCoy Pottery. $12.00 – 15.00.

Left: Turtle, 2¼" high. Marked Floraline #484, LCC, McCoy Pottery after Lancaster Colony took over. $9.00 – 12.00. Right: Sleeping turtle, 7". Marked Juanita Crooks, Cookson Pottery. $12.00 – 15.00.

Frog on mushrooms, 11½" tall. Unmarked. $18.00 – 22.00.

Left: Twin fish with starfish, 6" x
7¾". Unmarked. $10.00 – 12.00.
Right: Open-mouth fish, 4" tall.
Marked Italy 69/425. $6.00 – 9.00.

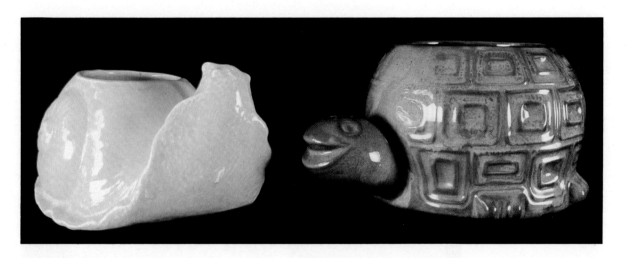

Left: Yellow snail, 4¼" x 7½". Unmarked. $7.00 – 9.00. Right: Box turtle, 4¼" x 8½". Marked McCoy #740, LC-USA.
$12.00 – 15.00.

Left: Snail, 4¼" tall. Lefton #H7436. $15.00 – 18.00. Right: Shell, 5" x 6¾". Frankoma Pottery.
Marked #575. $12.00 – 15.00.

Left: Fish, 4¼" long. Shawnee Pottery, USA. $6.00 – 8.00. Right: Bug (evidently the one the fish is after), 6¾" long. Marked R.R.P. CO. (Robinson-Ransbottom) #416. $15.00 – 20.00.

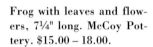

Frog with leaves and flowers, 7¼" long. McCoy Pottery. $15.00 – 18.00.

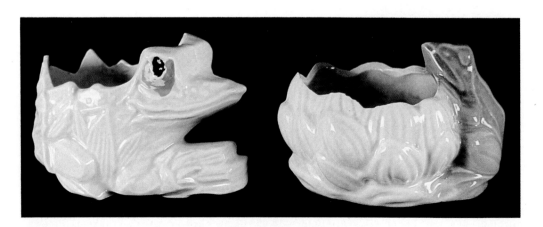

Left: Yellow frog, 5" long. McCoy Pottery, about 1949. $12.00 – 15.00. Right: Frog on lotus, 5" long. McCoy Pottery, about 1943. $12.00 – 15.00.

Left: Another McCoy frog, 5"
long. $12.00 – 15.00. Center:
Color variation of Shawnee fish.
$6.00 – 8.00. Right: Standing
turtle, 5½" tall. Brush McCoy.
$30.00 – 35.00.

Fish, 7½" x 9". Stanford Pottery. $12.00 –
15.00.

Whale, 5" x 9". Unmarked. $10.00 –
12.00.

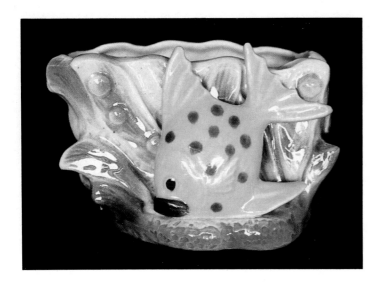

Swimming fish, 2¾" x 5". Marked H.P.
Wales China, Japan with black stamp.
$6.00 – 9.00.

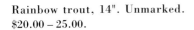
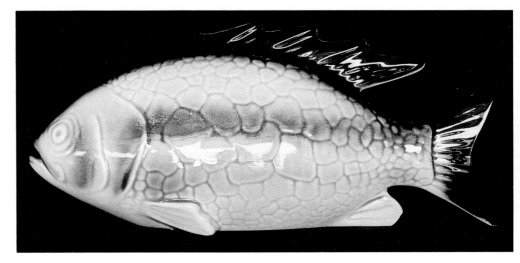

Rainbow trout, 14". Unmarked.
$20.00 – 25.00.

Left: Upright fish, 7" tall. Unmarked.
$8.00 – 10.00. Right: Seahorse, 7" tall.
Unmarked. $8.00 – 10.00.

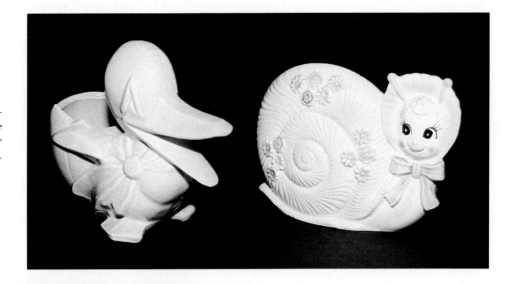

Left: Duck, 7" long. McCoy Pottery. $8.00 – 10.00. Right: Cute baby snail, 6¼" long. Sticker NAPCOWARE, Japan 8571. $6.00 – 9.00.

Left: Frog musician vase, 6¾" tall. Shawnee, USA. $18.00 – 20.00. Right: Strawberry vase with bird, 8¼" tall. McCoy Pottery introduced about 1949. $20.00 – 25.00.

Bird with fish, 11¾" long. Brush Pottery. $35.00 – 40.00.

Eagle with wing up, 11" long. Unmarked. Lovely piece! $20.00 – 25.00.

Left: Bird with nest, 6" tall. Brush Pottery. $15.00 – 18.00. Right: Eagle with wingspread of 8¼". Unmarked. $15.00 – 20.00.

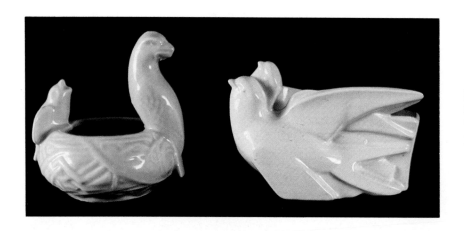

Left: Birds on nest, 5½". Marked only USA. Shawnee. $18.00 – 20.00. Right: White birds flying, 7¼". McCoy. $15.00 – 18.00.

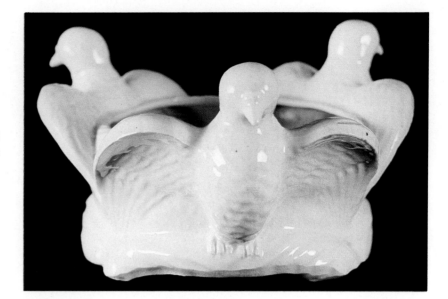

Triple birds, 7¼" diameter. Stamped Made in Japan. Seems like Japan likes things in threes. $10.00 – 12.00.

Bird on bowl, 10¼" long. McCoy Pottery. $18.00 – 22.00.

Left: Bird with flower, 5¼" x 7". Marked USA. Brush Pottery. $15.00 – 20.00. Right: Little bird on big bowl, 7½" long. Marked Knox Imperial Holiday with palm tree stamp. $8.00 – 10.00.

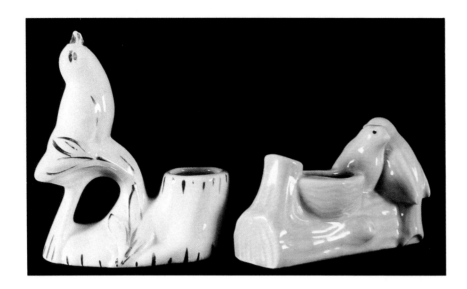

Left: Bird at stump, 7⅜" tall. Gold trim. Unmarked. $8.00 – 10.00. Right: Birds with nest, 6¾" long. Unmarked. $7.00 – 9.00.

Left: Small bowl with perching bird, 6" long. Royal Copley. $8.00 – 10.00. Right: Birdbath, 6" tall. McCoy Pottery, about 1949. $18.00 – 22.00.

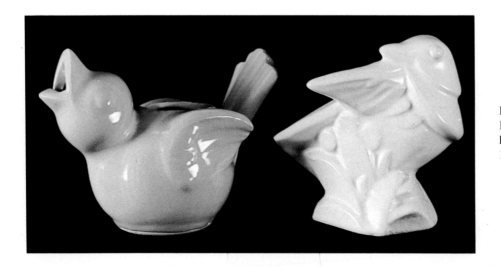

Left: Open mouth bird, 4" x 6". Shawnee Pottery. $7.00 – 10.00. Right: Preening bird, 4¾" tall. McCoy Pottery. $12.00 – 15.00.

Left: Parrot, 8¼" long. Unmarked. $10.00 – 12.00. Right: Pecking bird, 7½" long. Unmarked. $8.00 – 10.00.

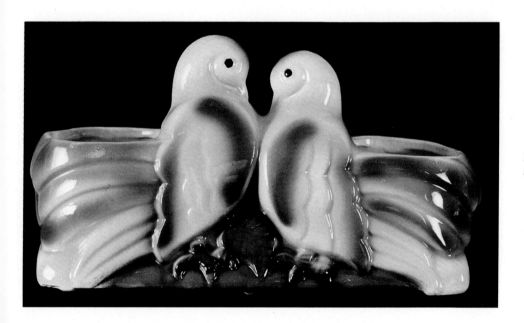

Lovebirds, 11¼" long. Unmarked. $12.00 – 14.00.

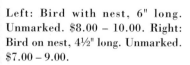

Left: Bird with nest, 6" long. Unmarked. $8.00 – 10.00. Right: Bird on nest, 4½" long. Unmarked. $7.00 – 9.00.

Left: Bird on blossom, 7¼" long. This is shown in both American Bisque and the Brush books. I say American Bisque. $12.00 – 14.00. Right: Goldfinches on nest, 8" long. Unmarked. $9.00 – 12.00.

Left: Parrot, 5" x 6". American Bisque. $12.00 – 15.00. Right: Turkey, 4½" tall. Morton Pottery. $9.00 – 12.00.

Left: Parrot, 6". Unmarked. $8.00 – 10.00. Right: Parrot at tub, 7⅝" tall. McCoy. Marked NM, USA. $12.00 – 15.00.

Pouter pigeon vase, 9". McCoy Pottery. $12.00 – 15.00.

Bird on log, 4¾". Unmarked. $9.00 – 12.00.

Left: Bluejay on stump, 5" tall. Red-stamped Made in Japan. $7.00 – 9.00.
Right: Pair of cardinals, 5½" tall. Sticker marked NAPCO Ceramics, Japan. $8.00 – 10.00.

Bluebird with rhinestone eyes, 6" tall. George Z. Lefton #288. $12.00 – 15.00.

Chick with open mouth, 5¼" long. Gold trim.
Unmarked. $7.00 – 9.00.

Parrot resting, 8" long. Unmarked. Probably
Morton Pottery. $9.00 – 12.00.

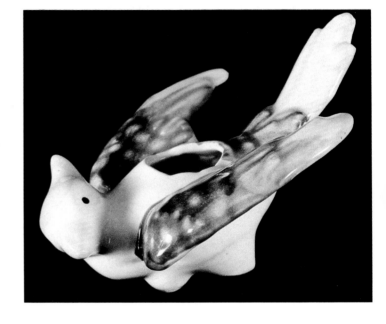

Spread-winged bird in wire cage. Metlox Pottery. $18.00 – 22.00.

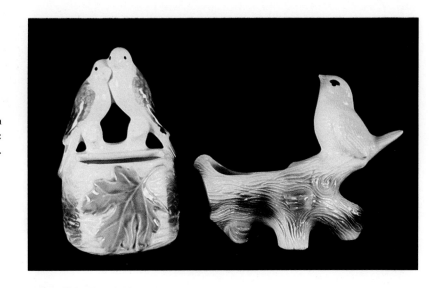

Left: Parakeet duo, 7" tall. Morton Pottery. $12.00 – 15.00. Right: Wren on tree truck, 5¾" x 7½". Royal Copley. $15.00 – 18.00.

Hanging parrot with plum blossoms, 6¾" diameter. Note hard-to-find bisque chain with hook on each end. Made in Japan. $20.00 – 25.00 alone; more with chain. This is from the 1940s.

Long-tailed bird, 11¾" tall. Base is hollow. Unmarked but lovely! $18.00 – 22.00.

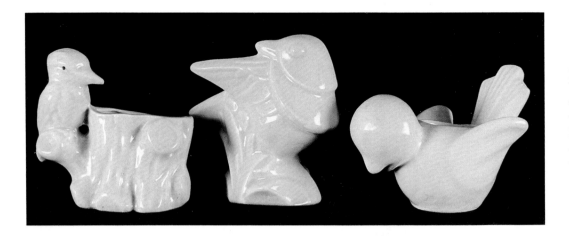

Left: Kingfisher on stump, 4".
Unmarked. $6.00 – 8.00.
Center: Preening bird, 4½"
tall. McCoy. $12.00 – 15.00.
Right: Bird with head down,
3⅝" tall. Shawnee Pottery.
$7.00 – 9.00.

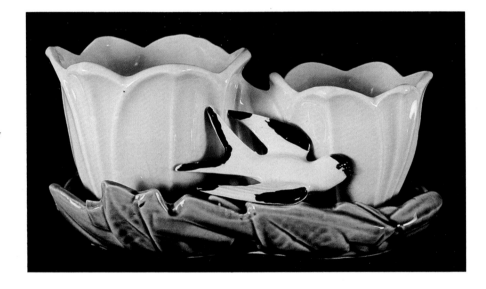

Double pot with bird, 10" long. McCoy
Pottery, about 1948. $15.00 – 18.00.

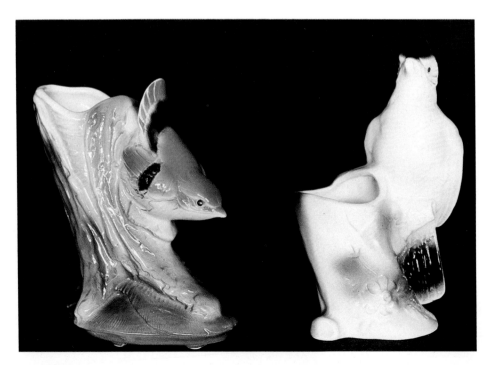

Left: Nuthatch planter, 5". Royal Copley. $10.00 – 12.00. Right: Woodpeck-
er planter, 6½" tall. Royal Copley.
$15.00 – 18.00.

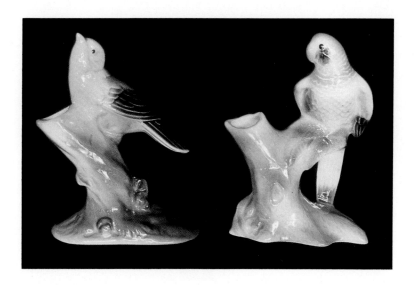

Left: Warbler bud vase, 5". Royal Copley. $10.00 – 12.00. Right: Parrot bud vase, 5" tall. Royal Copley. $10.00 – 12.00. I hear when these first came out, many folks used them for rooting cuttings of their favorite houseplants.

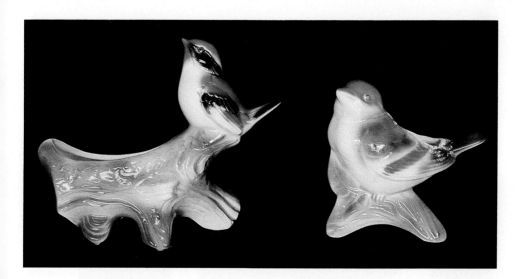

Left: Wren on tree stump, 6¼" x 8½". Royal Copley. $18.00 – 20.00. Right: Kinglet planter, 4½" tall. Royal Copley. $12.00 – 15.00.

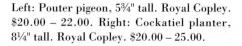

Left: Pouter pigeon, 5¾" tall. Royal Copley. $20.00 – 22.00. Right: Cockatiel planter, 8¼" tall. Royal Copley. $20.00 – 25.00.

Left: Dove at treetrunk, 7". Red-stamped Made in Japan. $12.00 – 15.00. Right: Finch vase, 5¾". Made in Czechoslovakia #20. $25.00 – 30.00. Another vase for rooting cuttings of plants.

Left: Woodpecker vase, 4½". Czechoslovakia. $35.00 – 40.00. Center: Stork vase, Czech. $40.00 – 45.00. Right: Tail up bird, Czech. $35.00 – 40.00.

Back view of Czech bird at left.

Large crested bird, 7¾". Czech. $45.00 –
50.00.

Left: Long-tailed bird, 4¼" x 6½". Czech. $40.00 – 45.00. Right: Woodpecker on tree, 5⅝" tall. Czech. $35.00 –
40.00.

Left: Bird on oak tree, 5¼". Czech. $35.00 – 40.00. Center: Finch on stump, 4¾" tall. Czech. $30.00 – 35.00. Right: Crested bird on stump, 5¼" tall. Czech. $35.00 – 40.00.

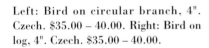

Left: Bird on circular branch, 4". Czech. $35.00 – 40.00. Right: Bird on log, 4". Czech. $35.00 – 40.00.

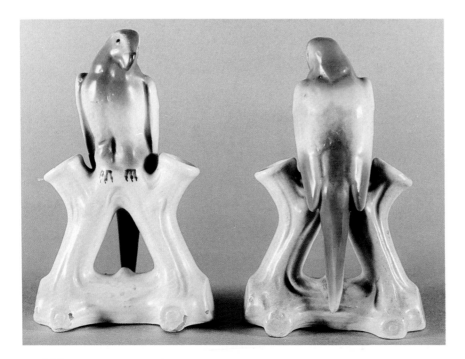

Parrot on triangular logs, 5¾". Same bird, different color combinations. Czech. $40.00 – 45.00.

Parrots on stump, 5½". Same bird, different colors. Czech. $35.00 – 40.00.

Left: Woodpecker on stump, 5¼". Czech. $35.00 – 40.00. Center: Bird on tree, 4¼". Czech. $35.00 – 40.00. Right: Long-tailed bird, 5" tall. Czech. $40.00 – 45.00.

Left: Bird on log, 3½" x 4½". Czech. $35.00 – 40.00. Right: Bird on log, 3½" x 4½". Czech. $35.00 – 40.00.

Parrots, 4¾". Same bird, different colors. Czech. $35.00 – 40.00.

Left: Warbler bud vase, 4¾". Royal Copley. $10.00 – 12.00. Center: Mother Goose, 3" tall. Shawnee Pottery. $8.00 – 10.00. Right: Singing bird, 4". McCoy Pottery, about 1943. $8.00 – 10.00.

Left: Raffish-looking toucan, 5½". Unmarked. $9.00 – 12.00. Right: Singing bird, 6¾". McCoy, about 1943. These came in several sizes and colors. $10.00 – 12.00.

Left: Color variations of the 6¾"
and 4¼ singing birds by McCoy
Pottery, about 1943. Left: $10.00
– 12.00. Right: $8.00. – 10.00.

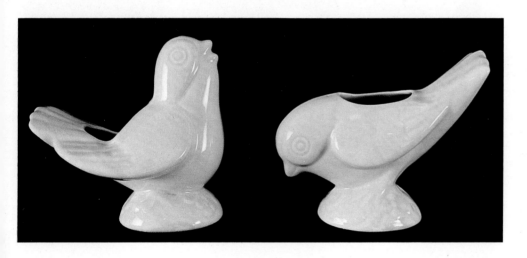

Singing bird, 5¼". Unmarked.
Somewhat like McCoy. $7.00 –
9.00. Right: Pecking bird, 5" tall.
Unmarked. $6.00 – 9.00.

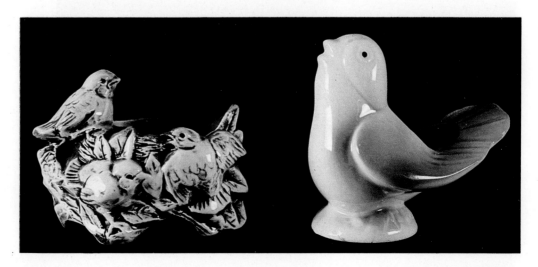

Left: Birds on nest, 5" long.
McCoy Pottery, about 1955.
$15.00 – 18.00. Right: 5" tall.
Another bird similar to McCoy.
Unmarked. $7.00 – 9.00.

Left: Rooster, 9" long. Looks like a studio piece, marked L. Dryden. $10.00 – 12.00. Right: Bluebird, 5¾" tall. RELPO. $10.00 – 12.00.

Left: Bird of paradise, 5". American Bisque. $18.00 – 20.00. Right: Hen and rooster, 3¾". Colors look like Royal Copley but no mark. $10.00 – 12.00.

Left: Rooster with pot, 6½". Unmarked. $7.00 – 9.00. Right: Rooster with corn, 6" x 6". American Bisque. $10.00 – 12.00.

Left: Rooster vase, 7¼". Royal Copley. $15.00 – 18.00. Right: Stuffed animal, 6". Royal Copley book lists as duck. $30.00 – 35.00.

Rooster, 7¾" tall. Royal Copley. What a handsome fellow! $30.00 – 35.00.

Left: Color variation of rooster with corn, 6¼". American Bisque. $10.00 – 12.00. Right: Rooster with wheelbarrow, 10". McCoy USA. $20.00 – 25.00.

Left: Owl on stump, 7¾" long.
Unmarked. $9.00 – 12.00.
Right: Owl on log, 8¼" long.
Unmarked. $9.00 – 12.00.

Owl face with bird on hat, 5½" tall x 7½"
diameter. This is a great piece signed by
sculptor Shepard Eberly. We found it in a
mall while photographing and although I did
not really collect planters myself (up until
then!) I HAD to have him! $40.00 – 45.00.

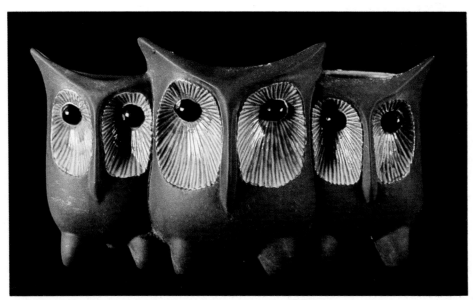

Owl trio, 8½" long. Marked Red Wing
USA. $18.00 – 22.00.

Left: Duck, 4¾". Brush Pottery. $20.00 – 25.00. Right: Owl, 6¼. Unmarked. $7.00 – 9.00.

Left: Pelican, 6" x 7¾". Unmarked. $8.00 – 10.00. Right: Perching owls, 5" x 5½". Fredericksburg Pottery. $12.00 – 14.00.

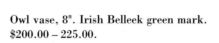

Owl vase, 8". Irish Belleek green mark. $200.00 – 225.00.

Left: Quail, 7" long. Japan. $7.00 – 9.00. Right: Owls next to stump, 7". Unmarked. $9.00 – 12.00.

Quail family, 7" x 9". McCoy Pottery, about 1955. $20.00 – 25.00.

Quail, 9¾" tall. American Art Pottery. $25.00 – 30.00.

Cock pheasant, 6" x 7¼". McCoy Pottery, about 1959. $20.00 – 25.00.

Dove-like bird basket drilled for hanging, 7¼" x 12". McCoy Pottery, marked LCC, USA, 1620. $20.00 – 22.00.

Pheasant, 14". Unmarked. Lovely detail. $15.00 – 20.00.

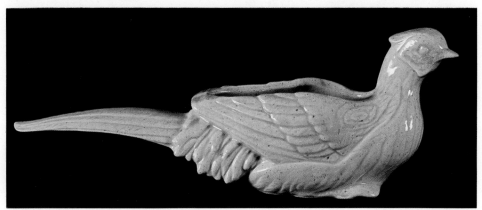

Pheasant, 8⅜" x 17". American Art
Potteries. $20.00 – 22.00.

Pheasant, 14". American Art Potteries.
A color and size variation of pheasant
above. $30.00 – 35.00.

Left: Goose, 5¾". Unmarked.
$5.00 – 7.00. Right: Quail, 5¼".
Unmarked. $5.00 – 7.00.

Left: Wings-up swan, 4½". American Bisque. $10.00 – 12.00. Right: Bird on stump, 4½". Unmarked. $7.00 – 9.00.

Left: Birds on fence, 4¼" x 5". Marked F & M Artware. $10.00 – 12.00. Right: Swan, 4½" long. American Bisque. $7.00 – 9.00.

Left: Cockatiel vase, 6". Unmarked. $7.00 – 9.00. Right: Wings-up duck, 5¼". Unmarked. $6.00 – 8.00.

Left: Parakeet, 6½". American Bisque. $12.00 – 15.00. Right: Duck, 6". Marked Artistic Gifts, Inc, Burbank, California, Made in Taiwan. $6.00 – 9.00.

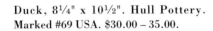

Duck, 8¼" x 10½". Hull Pottery. Marked #69 USA. $30.00 – 35.00.

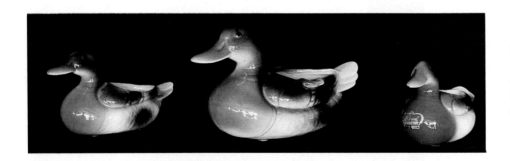

Royal Copley smoking set, as sold in stores. Center planter is 6¼" long, small trays 4½" long. Large: $15.00 – 18.00; small: $10.00. – 12.00.

Left: Mallard, 7½" x 11½". Unmarked. $7.00 – 9.00. Right: Mallard, 9½" tall. Marked China Craft. $8.00 – 10.00.

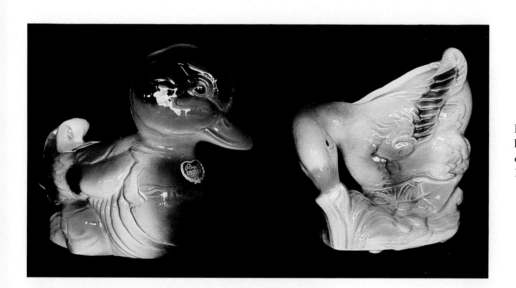

Left: Wood duck, 5½". Royal Copley. $15.00 – 18.00. Right: Gray duck, 5½". Royal Copley. $15.00 – 18.00.

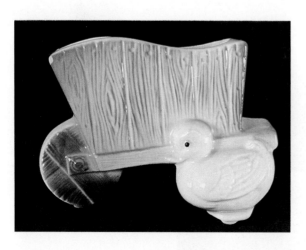

Duck and wheelbarrow, 5¼" long. Royal Copley. $18.00 – 20.00.

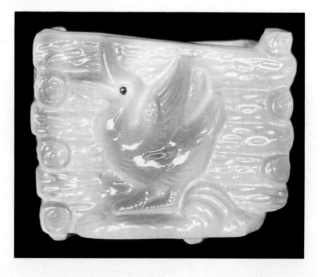

Duck on log wall, 4" x 4¾". Unmarked. $7.00 – 9.00.

Left: Mature wood duck, 7¼" tall.
Royal Copley. $20.00 – 25.00.
Right: Mallard duck, 8". Royal
Copley. $20.00 – 22.00.

Left: Pink swan, 7¾". Stanford
Pottery. $10.00 – 12.00. Right:
Cockatoo, 8½" x 10". Unmarked.
$15.00 – 18.00.

Left: Turkey, 7½". Unmarked.
$10.00 – 12.00. Right: Swan in
leaves, 6¾" x 11". American Bisque.
$25.00 – 30.00.

Left: Duck with bonnet, 6".
Unmarked. $6.00 – 9.00. Right:
Duck with leaf hat, 4". Japan. $6.00
– 8.00.

Left: Stork with baby, 7¼".
Unmarked. $7.00 – 9.00. Right:
Swan with shell, 5½" x 9".
Unmarked. $10.00 – 12.00.

Left: White and gold swan, 4¾".
Stanford Pottery. $12.00 – 15.00.
Right: Swimming mallard duck,
4¾" x 6½". American Bisque.
$18.00 – 22.00.

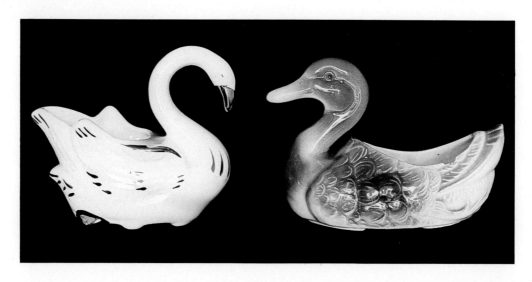

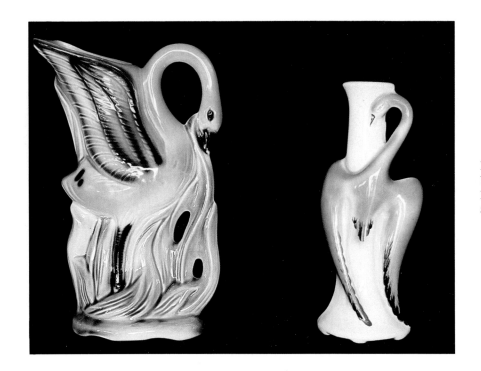

Left: Flamingo in leaves, 9¾".
Unmarked. $10.00 – 12.00. Right:
Flamingo vase, 8½". Unmarked.
$7.00 – 9.00.

Iridescent swan, 4¾" tall. Stanford Pottery. $20.00 – 25.00. Lovely color and
detail.

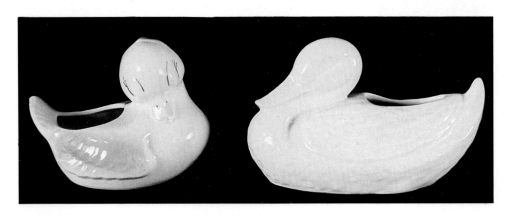

Left: Wood duck, 4¾" long.
Unmarked. $7.00 – 9.00. Right:
Duck, 6½" long. Marked only Made in
USA #944. $8.00 – 10.00.

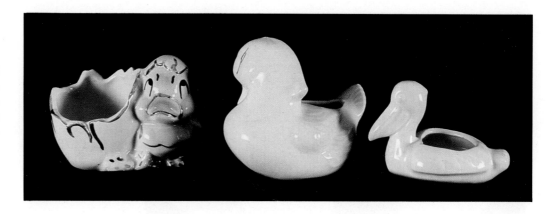

Left: Duck with egg, 3½". Gold trim. Unmarked. $6.00 – 9.00. Center: Wood duck, 4" x 5". Unmarked. $6.00 – 9.00. Right: Pelican, 3" tall. Unmarked. $5.00 – 7.00.

Goose with cart, 8" long. McCoy Pottery, about 1943. $15.00 – 18.00.

Left: Open-mouthed duck, 3¾" tall. McCoy Pottery. $5.00 – 7.00. Center: Swan, 3¾". Unmarked. $5.00 – 7.00. Right: Duck, 4½" tall. Brush-McCoy. $15.00 – 20.00.

Left: Duck, 5¼" tall. Brush. $20.00 – 25.00. Right: Duck just out of egg, 4¾". Unmarked. $7.00 – 10.00.

Left: Raised-wing swan with much gold trim, 7". Marked Shafer, 23K Gold, Guaranteed. $15.00 – 20.00. Right: Twin geese, 7¼" tall. Hull Pottery, 1950s. Marked USA #95. $45.00 – 50.00.

Duck decoy, 11½" long. Marked only with impressed P.3615. $15.00 – 18.00.

Brown duck with ribbon, 11½" long. Unmarked. $12.00 – 15.00.

Left: Bird with blossom, 4" x 5¾". American Bisque. $25.00 – 30.00. Right: Swan, 8" long. Frankoma Pottery marked #877. $12.00 – 15.00.

Left: Comic duck, 5". Unmarked. $6.00 – 8.00. Right: Goose, 4½". Brush Pottery. $20.00 – 22.00.

Swan planter/lamp combination, 12" tall.
Unmarked. Maddux of California, 1960s.
$15.00 – 18.00.

Preening swan, 9". Black-stamped Made in
Japan. $10.00 – 12.00.

Black swan, 8¾" long. Marked USA 802.
$12.00 – 15.00.

Long-necked swan, 12½" tall. Unmarked. $12.00 – 15.00. Flower decals and gold trim add to the value.

Left: Swan, 5¼". Gonder Pottery, marked E-44, USA. $20.00 – 22.00. Right: Flamingo, 6½" tall. Gold trim. Unmarked. $12.00 – 14.00.

Left: Pair of geese with applied flowers, 4¼" tall. Made in China sticker. Current. $7.00 – 9.00. Right: Preening goose, 6¾" x 7½". Unmarked. $7.00 – 9.00.

Flying duck planter, 8½" x 10½". McCoy Pottery, about 1955. $25.00 – 30.00.

Two swan vases by McCoy Pottery. "The Same Only Different." Left: 9½" tall, 8" at opening. Right: 9½" tall, 7" at opening. Vase on right is noticeably slimmer than one on left. $20.00 – 25.00.

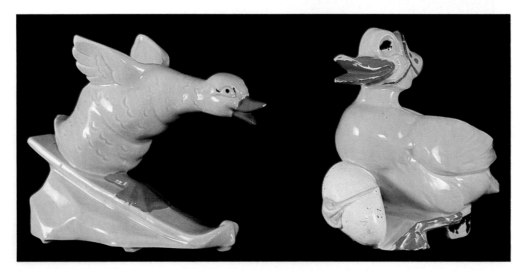

Left: Duck on snow board, 6¼" x 8¾". Unmarked. What a trip he's having – I love him! $15.00 – 18.00. Right: Standing duck with egg, 6½" x 7". McCoy Pottery, early 1950s. $18.00 – 22.00.

Left: Entwined swans, 7" tall. Camark Pottery USA 521. $30.00 – 35.00. Right: Swan with roses, 5½" tall. McCoy Pottery Antique Rose line, 1959. $18.00 – 22.00.

Left: Wing-up swan, 8". Haeger Pottery. $15.00 – 18.00. Right: Swan, 6¾" tall. McCoy Pottery, 1940s. $18.00 – 22.00.

Left: Duck with umbrella, 7¼" x 8½". McCoy Pottery, 1954. $35.00 – 45.00. Right: Duck on nest, 4¼" tall. Unmarked. $8.00 – 12.00.

Left: Duck, 6½" long. American Bisque. $7.00 – 9.00. Right: Brown duck, 10". Marked #830 USA. $7.00 – 9.00.

Left: Mallard duck, 6½". Product of Cash family's Clinchfield Artware Pottery. $7.00 – 9.00. Right: Duck in bonnet, 5" long. Unmarked. $7.00 – 9.00.

Mallard vase with handle, 9½" tall. Product of Cash family's Clinchfield Artware Pottery. Same piece was also made as pitcher. $12.00 – 18.00.

Left: Swan, 7⅝" tall. Haeger Pottery. Color variation of swan shown before. $12.00 – 14.00. Right: Goose, 5¾". Made in Taiwan. $7.00 – 9.00.

Left: Standing ostrich, 5¾". Brush Pottery. $18.00 – 22.00. Right: Sitting ostrich, 6½" tall. Brush Pottery. Marked #190. $20.00 – 25.00.

Left: Peacock, 6⅜" tall. Morton Potteries. Can be found in several colors. $7.00 – 9.00. Right: Standing ostrich, 5¾". Brush Pottery. Color variation. $18.00 – 20.00.

This unusual planter tilts to form either a penguin (top) or a rabbit (bottom). 6¾" tall. Unmarked. $20.00 – 25.00.

Three-headed dog, 7½" tall. Any way you look at him, he looks like a face with projecting ears. Marked only "Pat'd. 123112." $18.00 – 22.00.

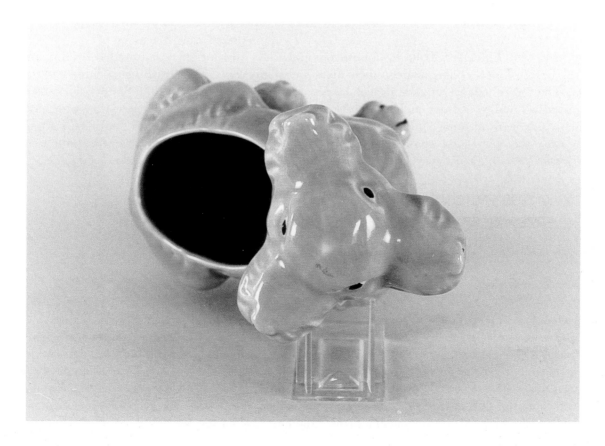

American Art Potteries

Located in Morton, Illinois, from 1946 – 1962. Founded by the four Rapp brothers, formerly of Midwest Potteries. Business began in a renovated garage building. The product was decorative or artware with unusual colors. The pottery ended in 1962 when it was sold for taxes.

American Bisque Company

Located in Williamstown, West Virginia, from 1919 – 1982. American Bisque began business making china doll heads which were becoming difficult to import since World War I. They then turned to the manufacture of various other products. Despite 10½ feet of water in the factory during a 1937 flood, and having the factory burn to the ground in 1945, American Bisque continued to make a great assortment of pottery items in huge quantities. In 1982 the company was sold to Bipin Mizra of American China Company. In 1983 the plant closed completely and all equipment was sold.

Brush-McCoy Pottery

Located in Roseville, Ohio, 1911 – 1925. Brush-McCoy came after the first Brush Pottery which operated from 1907 – 1908 and the J. W. McCoy Pottery which operated from 1899 – 1911. They made all sorts of kitchen and artware including many planters produced mainly in the late 1940s and 1950s. The name was changed to The Brush Pottery Company in 1925 and operated until 1982.

Clinchfield Artware Pottery

Located in Erwin, Tennessee, from 1945 until the mid 1980s the pottery was founded by Ray and Pauline Cash with the first few pieces being made in their home by mixing clays in the washing machine and firing pieces in the oven. They were makers of semi-porcelain decoratives and giftware. After Southern Potteries closed, Cash's acquired a number of their molds, mainly pitchers and character jugs. Since they also hand painted their products, this leads to some confusion between Clinchfield Artware pieces and Southern Potteries pieces. However, Cash's was very good about marking their pieces, which makes identification much easier. The "1945" mark was used on almost everything, whether the item was actually made in 1945 or not.

Czechoslovakian Pottery

If you remember your history and geography lessons, the Czechoslovakians and Slovaks lived in the section known centuries ago as Bohemia. In 1918, after WWI, the Czechs were awarded a country of their own named Czechoslovakia. Although this new country was very small, it was home to several hundred glass and china factories that exported great quantities to America. From 1948 – 1989 Czechoslovakia was Communist controlled; now there are two states—Czech Republic and Slovak Republic. Most, but not all, Czechoslovakian planters and vases will be found in a bisque finish or soft matt glaze. Generally clearly marked with ink stamps on the bottom or back of the piece, the most common being "Made in Czechoslovakia," red-stamped in a circle.

Florence Ceramics

Florence Ward began business with the manufacture of ceramic jewelry in the 1930s. Located in Pasadena, California, Florence made molded and hand decorated figurines during the 1940s and 1950s. In 1964, the business was sold to Scripto Company, which made more plebian items such as mugs, ashtrays, etc. The business closed around 1977.

Frankoma Pottery

Located in Sapulpa, Oklahoma, business began in 1936 and continues today. It was founded by John Frank who died in 1973, passing the reins to his daughter, Jonice Frank. Twice the pottery was nearly wiped out by fire but was rebuilt each time. Frankoma produced several very successful dinnerware lines as well as Christmas plates, sculptures and all types of novelty ware including planters. Oklahoma clay is used as a base for the pottery. With the addition of other earths, the pottery fires a brick red. The glazes are Rutile, which gives a soft, opaque glaze in shaded colors. The pottery is generally marked.

FRANKOMA POTTERIES

Fredericksburg Art Pottery

Located in Fredericksburg, Ohio, from 1910 – 1965, this pottery went through many changes of ownership, making mainly utilitarian and bath ware until 1939. At this time the plant was reorganized and began to make novelty items such as vases, cookie jars, planters, etc. In 1949, the plant was sold again to the Pilgrim Pottery Company. They continued the novelty line until the plant burned in 1965.

Haeger Potteries Inc.

Located in Dundee, Illinois, from 1871 when David H. Haeger purchased an interest in the Dundee Brick Yard. After 1900, his sons took over management and added flower pots to the line. In 1912 and 1914, they expanded and Haeger Potteries Inc. was born. Just before World War I, Haeger began its art pottery endeavors, sending a shipment to Marshall Field and Company in Chicago. In 1939, they took over the Macomb Pottery at Macomb, Illinois, and after that they continued to expand. In 1970 the Creek Indians built a pottery which was operated under Haeger's direction, and Cherokee Nation Pottery began. Many famous designers have worked for Haeger through the years. Haeger is still being produced.

Haeger   (Haeger)

Hull Pottery Company

In 1905, the A.E. Hull Pottery Company was founded in Crooksville, Ohio. In 1950 the plant suffered a fire that kept it closed until 1952. When it reopened, the initials in the name were left off and it became Hull Pottery Company. Art pottery was produced from 1917 until the early 1950s. All types of pottery pieces were produced until they closed in 1986. Most pieces were marked, using incised marks or raised marks built into the mold.

Japanese Ware

Many of the planters we find today, marked with Japanese logos or with the logos of various importers, date from the early 1900s onward. Occupied Japan pieces were produced from 1947 – 1952, and massive amounts were made and exported. Many pieces made both before and after the war were marked just "Japan," so dating is very difficult. Marks may be ink stamped or incised into the body of the clay.

Nelson McCoy Pottery

Nelson McCoy founded the Nelson McCoy Sanitary and Stoneware Company in Roseville, Ohio, in 1910. He died in 1945. He was succeeded by Nelson Melick McCoy until 1954, then Nelson McCoy, Jr., who resigned in 1981. In its heyday, McCoy was a huge pottery employing 300 people. All types of pottery were manufactured to the tune of five million pieces per year. After 1974, McCoy was owned by the Lancaster Colony Group. It was sold again in 1986. McCoy made many lovely and intricate planters and vases. Most of the pottery produced after 1938 is marked, although you may have to hunt to find it.

Metlox Pottery

Founded by T. C. Prouty in Manhattan Beach, California, in 1927. They originally made the ceramic part of neon signs. The production of dinnerware and artware began about 1938 but quickly halted as World War II began. Metlox began to make 90% factory production of machine parts for the duration. After the war, dinnerware production began again. Evan K. Shaw purchased the plant in 1947 and in 1958 Metlox bought the patterns and equipment from Vernon Kilns. Evan's son, daughter and son-in-law all worked together. Shaw died in 1980 and son-in-law Kenneth Avery and his wife took over management. Metlox ceased operations in 1989.

Morton Pottery Company

Morton was founded by the sons of Andrew Rapp, one founder of the Rapp Bros. Brick and Tile Company in Morton, Illinois. They began pottery making in 1923. Morton Pottery closed in 1976. Unfortunately, most of their planters and other items were not marked. Morton went through many name changes, fires and other trials during their years of production, but the Rapp family was always involved in the business somewhere.

Niloak Pottery Company

Located in Benton, Arkansas. In 1909 – 1910, owner Charles D. Hyten developed a swirled, hand-thrown art pottery known as "Mission Ware." This was made until the late 1930s. In the late 1920s, a less expensive line of solid colored ware was introduced. This was called "Hywood." This name was later dropped but any pieces that were marked carried the Niloak name. It is in the Hywood line that the planters are found. Niloak marks are ink stamped or impressed. Business ended about 1941.

NILOAK
NILOAK

Red Wing Potteries Inc.

Located in Red Wing, Minnesota, from 1936 – 1967. The company was founded in 1877 and went through several name and owner changes. Red Wing was a leader in the dinnerware field, but after World War II, the same fate that other American potteries endured caught Red Wing. The fatal blow came with a strike for higher wages by factory workers and Red Wing closed in 1967. They did not produce a great number of figural planters, but those that were made were of fine quality with imaginative workmanship. These were mainly made in the 1960s.

Royal Copley-Spaulding

Spaulding China Company made Royal Copley products. Morris Feinberg, president, founded Spaulding in Sebring, Ohio, in 1942. The pottery actually began in a garage on East Ohio Avenue, and moved to the abandoned Alliance Vitreous China Company plant, finding a home at last in the old Sebring Rubber Company. building. By 1947 or 1948, they were in production 24 hours a day, using a continuous circular kiln and were firing as many as eighteen thousand items a day. Royal Copley was produced during the entire life of Spaulding making up 85% of the company's entire production. Spaulding stressed design and quality at affordable prices and sold to Woolworth, Kresge, Grands and other chain stores across the country. Royal Copley made many, many lovely, high-quality planters and vases in figural and non-figural designs. Most are marked.

Robinson-Ransbottom Pottery Company

Located in Roseville, Ohio. Four Ransbottom brothers founded a pottery in Ironspot, Ohio, near Roseville around 1900. About 1920, they combined forces with Robinson Clay Products of Akron, and formed the Robinson-Ransbottom Pottery. Although pieces are generally clearly marked, folks have a tendency to confuse R.R.P. Co. products with those of the Roseville Pottery Company, simply because they both used the word "Roseville" in their marks. R.R.P. CO. is still in business today.

R. R. P. Co.
ROSEVIllE OHIO

Shawnee Pottery

The Shawnee Pottery was located in Zanesville, Ohio, from 1937 – 1961. It is said that one of the pottery stockholders found an arrowhead while walking over the factory grounds. He investigated and found that in the past, several Indian villages had been located in the area. The tribe that lived in these villages was Shawnee and he suggested the pottery adopt that name. The head of the company was Addis E. Hull, Jr., whose father founded the Hull Pottery Company of Crooksville, Ohio. Shawnee sold decorated pottery to S.S. Kresge Company, Woolworth's and Sears, among others. Some stores and jobbers designed their own pieces. Shawnee eventually became one of the most successful potteries in the country, but increased imports caught up with them, as with so many others, and they closed in 1961. Many of our lovely planters are products of Shawnee Pottery.

Stanford Art Pottery

Founded in Sebring, Ohio, by three Stanfords: George Sr., George Jr., and W. J. Stanford, plus L. L. Root in 1945. The company produced art pottery, lamp bases, giftware, and florist ware. In January 1961, the pottery was destroyed by fire but continued to operate in a selling capacity, according to *Lehner's Encyclopedia of U.S. Marks on Pottery, Porcelain and Clay.*

Importers, Jobbers and Decorators

Cardinal China Company—Located in Carteret, New Jersey, Cardinal was a distributor who used their own marks on decorative and kitchenware pieces made for them by other potteries. They were in business from the late 1940s onward.

ENESCO—Founded in 1959 in Milwaukee, Wisconsin, by Eugene Freedman. They were a branch of a wholesale merchandising catalog operation, the N. Shure Company. "N.S. Co." sounded like ENESCO, thus the name. In 1984, the company went international with headquarters in Elk Grove Village, Illinois. They distribute a myriad of giftware items and are in business today.

George Zoltan Lefton Company—Founded in 1940 by George Zoltan Lefton who was born in Hungary, the company is located in Chicago, Illinois. After coming to the U.S. in 1939, Lefton specialized in ceramics. After World War II, he began importing ceramic giftware from the Orient. Business now covers many different countries. They are a wholesale business only, distributing to gift and department stores.

INCARCO—International Artware Corporation, Cleveland, Ohio, formed by Irwin Garber in 1960-61. They were an importer of ceramic and glass florist ware and other giftware. In 1986, they were taken over by NAPCO and moved to Jacksonville, Florida.

Leeds China Company—Located in Chicago, Ilinois, this distributor was licensed by Disney to use their characters in various ceramic products including planters. They used a number of potteries to produce these items, so certain identification as to maker is very difficult.

NAPCO—National Potteries Corporation was founded in 1938 in Bedford, Ohio, by a Midwestern family. In the mid 1940s, Irwin Garber joined the company and later formed INARCO. In 1973-74 directories, the company was listed as being in Cleveland, Ohio. They are distributors of various decorative accessories, decorative glass, and novelty items.

Pearl China Company, East Liverpool, Ohio—In the mid 1930s, George Singer of the Pearl China Company, a selling operation, leased a pottery building from Hall China Company in order to expand his business. He began making art and novelty ware by the casting method and kept expanding until by the end of World War II, he employed 165 people. In 1958, the business was sold to Craft Master Corp. of Toledo, Ohio. Craft Master, in turn, was purchased by General Mills in 1968. In early 1973, the pottery part of the business was sold to Pioneer Pottery. A number of potteries made wares for Pearl China Company, including Homer Laughlin and Harker, along with many foreign companies. Many selling agencies had control over or owned their own potteries in those days so that the entire outpot of that pottery would go through a certain sales agency or jobber.

Pearl China Company is now a selling operation only and exists today as a gigantic outlet for all types of pottery. Pearl China Company marks may be found on many pottery pieces today, everything from decorative pieces to kitchenware and dinnerware. No marks have been used for many years now, however, because of the cost involved in backstamping. (Information from Lois Lehner's **U.S. Marks on Pottery, Porcelain & Clay**.)

RELPO—Reliable Giftware and Pottery Company, Chicago, Ilinois. They are importers listed in directories from 1950 to the present. Usually marked with a sticker or sometimes a black stamped mark.

Shafer, G. C. Pottery Company—Located in Zanesville, Ohio, 1930-1980. Shafer was a decorator working out of a small shop in the rear of his home. He owned his own molds that other companies used to make the ware that Shafer decorated with gold, decals, and overglaze. This mark was stamped on most pieces:

Shafer	DECORATED BY
23K Gold	G. C. SHAFER
Guaranteed	ZANESVILLE, OHIO

UCAGO — United China and Glass Company, Inc. Founded by Abe Mayer in 1850 as Abe Mayer & Company. In 1908, it was reorganized by J. W. Moses, Mayer's nephew, and was called United Glass & China Company, Inc. In 1935, the trademark UCAGO began being used. The business continues today under Sammons Enterprises, who purchased the business in 1956.

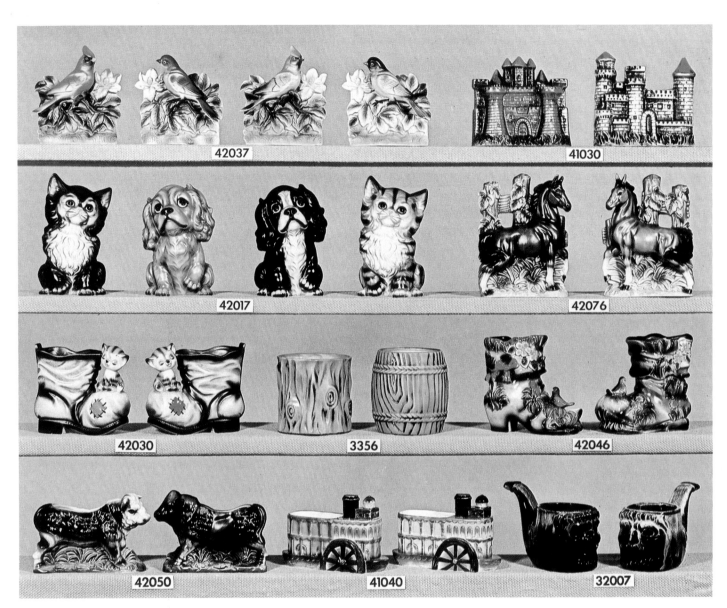

42037

41030

42017

42076

42030

3356

42046

42050

41040

32007

UCAGO catalog, 1966.

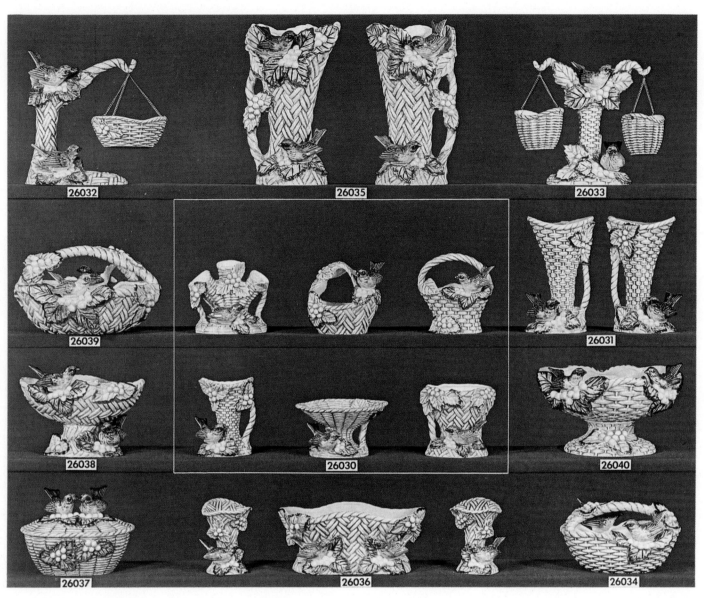

UCAGO catalog, 1966.

UCAGO catalog, 1966.

PEARL CHINA & POTTERY CO. East Liverpool, Ohio
"DISTINCTIVE PLANTERS"
Leakproof

D10 BEAR

D14 DUCK

D12 CAT

D13 ELEPHANT

D9 LAMB

D11 DOG

653 LAMB

497 BABY BOTTLE

D8 RABBIT

499 HORSE

3046 SWAN

Form 209

Pearl China & Pottery Co.

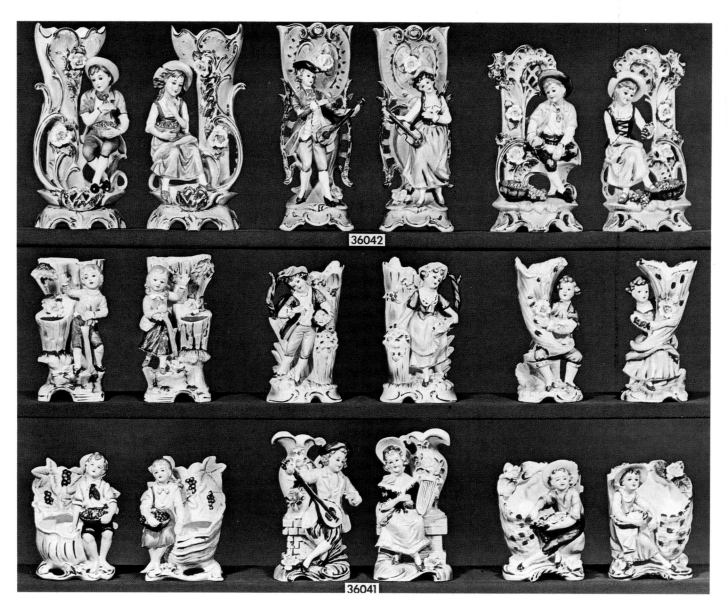

36042

36041

UCAGO catalog, 1966.

ARTWARE SPECIALS
SPECIAL NET PRICES
No Freight Allowance on these Items

AVAILABLE AS FOLLOWS:
Packed 2 dozen to a carton.
Each carton contains one color.
Available in #43 White or #42 Green

NOVELTY PLANTERS

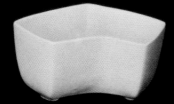

869 — planter, 8" across, .40 net

867 — planter, 5" across, .50 net

905 — Donkey Planter, 6" long,
Tan-Blue Trim, 3.25

868 — low bowl, 9" across, .50 net

893 — Donkey Planter, 8" long,
Brown-White Trim, 3.25

836 — oblong planter,
8½" across, .50 net

835 — low bowl, 10" across, .50 net

904 — Owl Planter,
3¼" across, 2.00

834 — compote planter, 6" high, .70 net

833 — round planter,
4" high, .50 net

897 — Owl Planter, 8¼" long,
Brown-White Trim, 3.50

917 — Lion Planter, 13" long,
Tahitian Gold, 3.50

906 — Dachshund Planter, 12½" long
40 — Cocoa Brown, 3.25

RED WING POTTERIES, INC. • RED WING, MINNESOTA

Red Wing catalog, 1963.

NOVELTY PLANTERS · GIFT ITEMS

907 — Violin Planter
14½" high, Rust, 3.25

908 — Banjo Planter
15" high, White, 3.25

896 — Giraffe Planter, 11" tall,
Brown with Tan Fleck, 4.50

COLONIAL DEEP-DISH PIE PLATE

Handsome in glowing brown earthenware, this 9 inch, deep-dish pie plate is a unique gift item. The original recipe for famous Hiawatha Valley Apple Custard Pie is on the label. Gift boxed. 1.50

**SINGLE-TIERED PLATE
ASSORTED PATTERNS, 2.20**

COOKIE JARS

BOB WHITE, 4.50

**FONDUE CASSEROLE &
WARMER STAND**

This 2½ quart Fondue is a lustrous brown with Village Green interior, the warmer stand in matching brown. Genuine Swiss Fondue recipe and rules for the Fondue Fun Game are on the label. Individually boxed, with warmer stand and candle. 7.95

**TWO-TIERED PLATE
ASSORTED PATTERNS, 4.00**

Set of 4 Ind.
Salad Bowls
Tan Fleck
4.00 Set

SALAD SET — TAN FLECK
2.70

#446 NUT OR RELISH TRAY
TAN FLECK
2.00

HAPPY, 4.50

RED WING POTTERIES, INC. • RED WING, MINNESOTA

Red Wing catalog, 1963.

Bibliography

American Bisque Catalog, 1956.

Coates, Pamela. *The Real McCoy Vol. I*. Des Moines, IA: Wallace-Homestead, 1971.

Coates, Pamela. *The Real McCoy Vol. II*. Indianapolis, IN: Self-published, 1974.

Garmon, Lee and Doris Frizzell. *Collecting Royal Haeger*. Paducah, KY: Collector Books, 1989.

Giacomini, Mary Jane. *American Bisque Collector's Guide*. Atglan, PA: Shiffer Publishing, 1994.

Gibbs, Carl Jr. *Collector's Encyclopedia of Metlox Potteries*. Paducah, KY: Collector Books, 1995.

Hall, Doris & Burdell. *Morton Potteries: 99 Years*. Gas City, IN: L&W Book Sales, 1995.

Huxford, Sharon & Bob. *The Collector's Encyclopedia of Brush-McCoy Pottery*. Paducah, KY: Collector Books, 1978.

Huxford, Sharon & Bob. *The Collector's Encyclopedia of McCoy Pottery*. Paducah, KY: Collector Books, 1978.

Lehner, Lois. *Lehner's Encyclopedia of U.S. Marks on Pottery, Porcelain and Clay*. Paducah, KY: Collector Books, 1988.

Mangus, Jim and Bev. *Shawnee Pottery*. Paducah, KY: Collector Books, 1994.

Nelson McCoy Catalogs, 1956, 1975.

Roberts, Brenda. *The Collector's Encyclopedia of Hull Pottery*. Paducah, KY: Collector Books, 1980.

Schneider, Mike. *Royal Copley Identification & Price Guide*. Atglan, PA: Shiffer Publishing Ltd., 1995.

Simon, Dolores. *Shawnee Pottery*. Paducah, KY: Collector Books, 1979.

Stanford Ware Catalog, 1959.

Supnik, Mark. *Collecting Shawnee Pottery*. Coral Springs, FL: Self published, no date.

UCAGO Catalog, 1966.